Praise for
Living the Quaker Way

"Anybody who has ever thought that the Quakers invented oatmeal will learn differently from *Living the Quaker Way* by Indiana pastor and highly readable author Philip Gulley. He describes the values of the Quaker way: simplicity, peace, integrity, community, and equality. Gulley is published by the new Random House imprint Convergent, which aims at people in the growing ranks of the spiritually curious but religiously unaffiliated."

—*Publishers Weekly* Top 10 in Religion, Fall 2013

"Ever since I 'discovered' Quakerism, I've wondered why Quakers are so quiet about their core values—simplicity, peace, integrity, community, and equality—in a world that so clearly needs them. So I was thrilled to find this book by Phil Gulley, a great Quaker writer, aimed at making those values more accessible. Gulley makes no effort to convince the reader to become a Quaker. He simply says, 'If you've been looking for ways to live out these values, here's what Quakers have learned over three and a half centuries of dedicated experimentation.' His book is a treasure trove of practical wisdom about what it means to bear witness to our hope for a better world."

—PARKER PALMER, author of *Healing the Heart of Democracy, Let Your Life Speak,* and *The Courage to Teach*

"*Living the Quaker Way* is not only refreshing and inspiring, it is challenging in all the right ways. Even though I am not a Quaker, their core values challenge my real life as well as the life of the faith community that I pastor. Filled with honest stories, deep wisdom, and realistic practices, *Living the Quaker Way* will leave you not only longing to live differently but also with practical ways to do just that."

—KATHY ESCOBAR, co-pastor of The Refuge, faith blogger, and author of *Down We Go: Living Into the Wild Ways of Jesus*

"This is nothing less than the gospel itself. Quakers have always had the ability to simplify and get to the point, and here it is! I am most happy to add my very positive endorsement to this excellent, clear, and much-needed book."

—FR. RICHARD ROHR, OFM, Center for Action
and Contemplation, Albuquerque, New Mexico

Praise for
Phil Gulley

"Philip Gulley separates wheat from chaff, experience from explanation, and purpose from function in this book. He calls the Jesus message into a new vision—one that has both power and integrity."

—JOHN SHELBY SPONG, former bishop of the Episcopal
Diocese of Newark and author of *The Sins of Scripture*

"No one raises provocative questions about Christianity more kindly than Philip Gulley."

—DIANA BUTLER BASS, author of *Christianity After Religion*
and *A People's History of Christianity*

"In our ever changing world, Gulley's book is much needed. An important book for any person of faith."

—ARCHBISHOP DESMOND TUTU

"The verve and clarity of Gulley's writing underscore the welcome nature of his message to many thoughtful unchurched or alienated Christians."

—*Library Journal*

Living
the
Quaker
Way

Living the Quaker Way

Timeless Wisdom for a Better Life Today

PHILIP GULLEY

CONVERGENT

LIVING THE QUAKER WAY
PUBLISHED BY CONVERGENT BOOKS

Details in some anecdotes and stories have been changed to protect the identities of the persons involved.

Hardcover ISBN 978-0-307-95578-4
eBook ISBN 978-0-307-95580-7

Cover design by Mark D. Ford

Published in the United States by Convergent Books, an imprint of the Crown Publishing Group, a division of Random House LLC, New York, a Penguin Random House Company.

CONVERGENT BOOKS and its open book colophon are trademarks of Random House LLC.

Library of Congress Cataloging-in-Publication Data
Gulley, Philip.
    Living the Quaker way : timeless wisdom for a better life today / Philip Gulley.
       pages cm
    ISBN 978-0-307-95578-4 (hardback) — ISBN 978-0-307-95580-7 (electronic)
 1. Christian life—Quaker authors. I. Title.
    BX7731.3.G85 2013
    248.4'896—dc23
                                                    2013012155

Printed in the United States of America
2013—First Edition

10 9 8 7 6 5 4 3 2 1

SPECIAL SALES
Most Convergent books are available at special quantity discounts when purchased in bulk by corporations, organizations, and special-interest groups. Custom imprinting or excerpting can also be done to fit special needs. For information, please e-mail SpecialMarkets@ ConvergentBooks.com or call 1-800-603-7051.

CONTENTS

Discovering Your Inner Quaker

It is not unusual in my neck of the woods to drive down an Indiana road and happen upon an old Quaker meetinghouse,* set back from the road with a cemetery nearby. The graves will date from the early 1800s to the current day, bookending the span of Quakerism in America's heartland. Many meetinghouses date from the mid-1800s. Given their age and the unintended message of death every graveyard conveys, passersby could be forgiven for believing Quakerism to be an antiquated tradition, out of step with the modern world.

---

* A Quaker house of worship is called a meetinghouse. A Quaker congregation is, therefore, called a meeting. A Quaker worship service is called a meeting for worship.

I know this misperception is a common one, for I believed it myself before becoming a Quaker; and others, who eventually became Quakers, also thought it true and told me so. To discover people still gather at those meetinghouses each Sunday, still laugh and love and learn within those serene spaces, is a surprise to those of us who believed Quakerism to be a dying expression. Not only is the mere existence of Quakerism a surprise, so are its vitality and relevance.

What is more surprising is that a religious tradition as evangelically bashful as Friends* is still around at all. The average Quaker, if there is such a thing, will warmly welcome a visitor once he or she arrives at a meetinghouse but would seldom have invited that person in the first place, fearing that might be construed as spiritually coercive or pushy. Instead, we rely upon our history and reputation—and in more recent years a website called Beliefnet.com—to evangelize for us. I first visited that website several years ago and was invited to answer a series of questions in order to determine the religion that best suited me. Intrigued, I took the quiz, submitted my answers for evaluation, and was informed I would feel most at home in a Quaker meeting. I remember chuckling to myself, pleased the test confirmed the path I had chosen over thirty-five years before.

A few weeks later, a visitor arrived at our Quaker meeting-

---

* The formal name for Quakers is the Religious Society of Friends. The term *Quaker* was at first a term of derision, soon adopted by Friends, who "trembled at the word of the Lord," according to George Fox, our founder.

house. After welcoming her, I asked if she had ever attended a Quaker meeting.

She answered, "No, this is my first time. But I took a test on the Internet, and it told me I'd be happy as a Quaker."

I mentioned I had taken the same test and had been told the same thing. Many others have visited our meetinghouse since, telling the same story. This has not been unique to our meeting. In my conversations with other Quakers around the country, they have reported the same phenomena. I would later learn a significant number of the quiz respondents were advised to consider Quakerism. This confirmed a long-held suspicion of mine—*there are far more people who embrace our Quaker traditions, testimonies, and beliefs than ever join a Quaker meeting.* Indeed, were everyone who is philosophically sympathetic to our tradition to join our ranks, ours might be the largest denomination in America.

Because so many people were advised by Beliefnet.com to consider Quakerism, I thought perhaps a Quaker had designed the test and was using it to expand our ranks, but that turned out not to be the case. Instead, I learned many people were sympathetic to the ideals of Quakerism without realizing their convictions were shared by a somewhat obscure religious faith over 350 years old. They were Quakers but didn't know it.

These newcomers to Quakerism have defied easy categorization. Some have been young, others elderly. Some have been prosperous, some have struggled economically. While most have had some experience with organized religion, their experience has been broad, ranging from Roman Catholicism to Judaism to Islam to Baptist. More than a few have been agnostics, uncertain about God but appreciative of the Quaker witness to peace and social justice. Several have mentioned finding the Quaker emphasis on silent reflection helpful to their spiritual journey. One man who had lived for some time in Asia said to me, "Quakerism might be America's closest thing to Buddhism."

I'm not sure what to make of our newfound popularity, but I am excited the long-held priorities of Quakerism are being valued by others and hope it signals a wider commitment to the virtues we Friends have cherished and practiced for centuries. At first, I worried the growing attraction of Quakerism was a fad and would fade over time. But as I engage those drawn to the Religious Society of Friends, I am sensing other motivations. They do not perceive Quakerism as fashionable or chic. *Rather, they have found its focus on the inner life to be an antidote to the complexities and challenges of modern life.* The Quaker values, what we call testimonies—simplicity, peace, integrity, community, and equality—offer an ethical and spiritual platform upon which people can happily build their lives.

It is this platform, this spiritual structure, I wish to explore in the pages ahead. These Friendly testimonies are easily remembered by the acronym SPICE: simplicity, peace, integrity, community, and equality. I would be remiss in suggesting these are uniquely Quaker ideals. They were not invented by us, and people of other faiths—or no faith at all—have lived them out powerfully and creatively. But I do believe these values are best honed in the crucible of community, which is why I remain a Friend. That these priorities speak to so many people today, including many who have scant knowledge of Quakerism, indicates the common ground shared by ancient traditions and modern seekers. We need not jettison the time-tested truths of our ancestors, but we do need to reinterpret them for our age, lest we mistake stale forms for vital living. It is then, with deep appreciation for the past and profound hope for our future, that I offer these testimonies of the Quaker way for your consideration.

But let me be clear, were I merely to inform you of this way, my job would be left undone. It is the life, *the Quaker way,* I urge you to take up and live. By that I do not mean for you to seek out the nearest Quaker meeting and become a member, though you may if you wish. I mean for you to embrace these values, to give your assent and your heart to these virtues, so that our world might be transformed. My interest is not in growing the Quaker denomination. My passion is in growing a world in which peace, love, and justice reign.

In the end, I am not inviting you to a church but to a life.

What Is a Quaker?

A man once e-mailed to tell me he had grown up in a traditional Christian church in the South but as an adult had become spiritually disillusioned and was exploring other religions. In the midst of his search, he had read a book I had written and become intrigued with Quakerism. His e-mail concluded by asking me if there were a Quaker meeting in his community he might attend. I went online to Quakerfinder.org, entered the name of his town, and discovered the closest Friends meeting to him was seventy-five miles away. So I encouraged him to begin a Quaker worship group in his home.

For a variety of reasons, he was unable to do that, though he continued to be intrigued by the Quaker way. Our correspondence went forward, driven by his curiosity about Quakerism. After many months and questions, he wrote, saying, "If someone asks me what religion I am, can I tell them I'm a Quaker, or do I need someone's permission?"

It was an intriguing question, inspiring me to think further about what it meant to be a Quaker.

Had my friend wished to become Roman Catholic, he would have had to attend a specific Catholic parish and enroll in a process called the Rite of Christian Initiation for Adults where, with other potential converts, he would have undertaken a series of lessons and liturgical rites that would eventually culminate in his confirmation, baptism, and membership in the Roman Catholic Church. It would be, as you can imagine, a precise and lengthy process intending to steep the convert in the history and doctrine of the Roman Catholic tradition.

On the other end of the ecclesial spectrum, had my friend wished to become a Unitarian Universalist, he would have attended a local UU congregation and signed the membership book. Depending on the congregation, he might first have had to take a class on that movement's history and beliefs, but in some congregations it wouldn't have been required. Indeed, in some UU congregations, he could have signed the membership book on his first visit. If there had been no Unitarian Universalist church in his community, he could have gone online, clicked a button, and joined the Church of the Larger Fellowship, the Unitarian Universalist's virtual community. He could then have proudly identified himself as a Unitarian Universalist in good standing, even though he knew little about the denomination.

Had he wished to join a Quaker meeting in my own yearly meeting,* he would theoretically have had to profess his faith in Jesus Christ, accept the principles of Christianity as held by Quakers, and share in the financial obligations of the meeting. I say "theoretically" because there isn't a shared consensus in my yearly meeting about what it means to have faith in Jesus Christ. This ambiguity is a source of consternation to some Friends and has resulted in several Friendly clashes over the centuries.

While Quakers are typically organized into larger bodies, very few of those associations enforce a standard of membership. Neither do we have a pope or president who can impose criteria for membership. Nor is there is an assembly of bishops or clerics who can compel persons to believe certain tenets before membership is granted. To be sure, Quakers once observed strict rules governing membership, marriage, conduct, appearance, behavior, and beliefs, and felt free to "read out of meeting," or expel those Friends who violated the expected norms. But those days are long past and are now viewed with some embarrassment.

This is all to say that no Quaker body, council, or leader exists who could say to my friend, "You are not a Quaker." If one were a stickler about such matters, he or she might say to my friend, "You must be a member of a Quaker meeting to say you

---

* *Yearly meeting* is the term given to the Quaker congregations in a geographic region who gather once a year to discuss and act upon their mutual ministries and concerns. I am a member of Western Yearly Meeting, headquartered in Plainfield, Indiana, consisting of Quaker meetings in the western half of Indiana and the eastern half of Illinois.

are a Quaker." But many who worship at a Friends meeting, though they have not formally joined that body, still view themselves, and are considered by others, as Friends.

While those who value formality might find this lack of ceremony unsettling, it is entirely consistent with the Friends' tendency of valuing inward convictions over outward rituals. To the Quaker, sincere dedication is preferred to public declarations that may or may not be earnest. This is why we have eschewed sacramental religion, for in the back of our minds lurks the fear that rituals and words might in repetition become empty.

> To the Quaker, sincere dedication is preferred to public declarations that may or may not be earnest.

This is all to say that if one claims to be a Quaker and sincerely endeavors to live out the principles of Friends, his or her lack of membership in a Quaker community would not be a sticking point with most Friends. Those Quakers who would challenge another's standing would have to explain how the outward ritual of joining a meeting is superior to one's inward commitment to the Quaker way, a difficult task in a religion that prizes inward dedication above outward declaration.

Were I authorized by all Friends (a most unlikely circumstance) to define what it meant to be a Quaker, I would speak about a lifestyle that highlights the values I believe are central to Quakerism, while hastening to note that other Friends might see matters differently. The historic schisms among Friends, and there are several, bear witness to the passionate differences among us. These differences include our understanding of the nature of Jesus, the role and authority of Scripture, patterns of worship, participation in sacraments, the value of ecumenism and religious tolerance, issues involving pastoral leadership and governance, the peace testimony, homosexuality and same-gender marriage, and the degree to which God is (or isn't) emphasized, not to mention our lack of consensus about God's nature and objectives.

While our earliest decades in the mid-1600s were marked with a surprising uniformity of thought and practice, Friends would eventually, even eagerly, strike out in new directions, inspired by their sense of divine leading. Some would actively resist and reject war; others would not. Some would labor to free slaves; others would own them. Some would preach and travel widely; others would remain in their communities. Some would charitably engage persons of other faiths; others would associate only with fellow Friends. This diversity should come as no surprise given Quakerism's start as a reaction against the organized church of the day. Spiritual revolution is a difficult animal to tame, and individual Friends would inevitably be inclined to follow their own paths.

This makes the seemingly simple questions, What is a Quaker? or What do Quakers believe? almost impossible to answer, which is why I favor a more fluid definition for fear of excluding someone who would, as I do, claim that label. Quakerism, like many religions that came of age in America, reflects our country's wide diversity. This theological elasticity enables us to include in our ranks a traditional fifth-generation midwestern farmer and also a college-aged spiritual seeker who freely roams the world's religions. People of diverse backgrounds and beliefs find their spiritual home in contemporary Quakerism. This is at once our greatest strength and the chief source of our

> Despite our differences, most all of us agree that to be a Quaker is to live out as best we can the virtues of simplicity, peace, integrity, community, and equality.

family squabbles. Unlike the Amish, with whom we are often mistakenly confused, Friends do not look alike, think alike, or believe alike. Despite our differences, most all of us agree that to be a Quaker is to live out as best we can the virtues of simplicity, peace, integrity, community, and equality.

A Way of Life or a Religion?

While attending a summer gathering of Friends at a college, I found myself unable to sleep in the warm dormitory room I'd been assigned, so I went downstairs to the air-conditioned lobby where I found a small group of Friends also escaping the heat. We began talking about the day's events and soon fell into a spirited conversation that led to a good-natured disagreement.

In the middle of our debate a woman entered the lobby. One of the Friends said, "We'll let Mary settle it!"

"Settle what?" Mary asked.

"Is Quakerism a way of life or a religion?" the Friend asked. "I say it is a religion, but these Friends say it is a way of life."

"It is both," Mary said. "It is a way of life rooted in our experience of God."

I agreed with Mary, thinking to myself, one couldn't be a Quaker without also believing in God. A few months later, I met several Friends who identified themselves as atheists. Initially, I thought they were rejecting an image of God they had been taught as children. Many of us do that, eventually arriving at an understanding of God that resonates with our spiritual experiences. But when I engaged these atheists in conversation, I learned their atheism went far beyond their disquiet with a specific childhood image of the Divine. They could not affirm the existence of a Divine Presence they had never personally experienced. They struck me as highly moral people working diligently to better the world. But their sense of integrity would not permit them to claim a relationship to a Divine Presence they had not encountered.

While my practice of Quakerism is rooted in my experience of God, that is not the case for all Quakers. For some Friends—

indeed for most Friends—Quakerism is first a religion, an understanding and experience of God that leads to a certain way of life. But for others it is a way of life rich in its own right, needing no origin in or confirmation from a divine entity. To the question, "Is Quakerism a way of life or a religion?" I would answer, "It depends upon the Quaker." This dual reality explains the wide diversity among Friends today. For some, Quakerism is a religion, a way of comprehending and relating to God, usually through the life and witness of Jesus. But that is not all it is. For the atheist Friend, Quakerism is a way of living in the world so that the world is made more just, loving, and peaceable by his or her presence.

It is not my place to say one understanding of Quakerism is superior to another. The God I believe in is happy to work anonymously, neither requiring nor demanding recognition for every act of human kindness.

The next time I see Mary, I might suggest to her that while Quakerism for some Friends is a way of life rooted in our experience of God, that is not the case for all. At one time, I would have mightily resisted that view, but now I am quite willing to welcome as brother and sister those persons whose integrity will not permit them to affirm a god they have not encountered. Though our perceptions of the Divine may differ, our mutual commitment to the Quaker way allows us to stand with one another as Friends and friends. It is this Quaker way—the way of simplicity, peace, integrity, community, and equality—I wish to explore in the pages ahead.

Simplicity

For several summers, my wife and I traveled to northern Michigan for a week's stay at a United Methodist Chautauqua, Bay View, near the small town of Petoskey. Though I had been engaged to speak each day, the schedule allowed us ample time for long walks and reading, our favorite hobbies. By the end of the week, we were well rested and reluctant to return home, where the daily responsibilities of life awaited us. While driving home, we reflected on our time together, remembering aloud some of the finer moments of our trip. We concluded that the absence of telephones and other media had contributed to our sense of peace. We had unplugged the television and radio, turned off our cell phones, and taken the house telephone off the hook. The cottage in which we stayed had a welcoming front porch and much of our time was spent there, napping, reading, and visiting with passersby.

Even though I tend to avoid electronic distractions, it is nearly impossible to do so without becoming Amish. But even some of the Amish, I have noticed, now carry cell phones, disrupting their once simple lives. Though my wife and I live without television, we have been unable to escape the intrusive claims of other media and electronics. We feel tethered to our cell phones; we check our e-mail frequently, sometimes addictively. Our favorite time of the week has become Sunday morning, when we can enter our simple Quaker meetinghouse and sit in silence, undisturbed by the clamor and demands of modern life.

When I first became a Quaker in my teenage years, I never dreamed I would grow fond of simplicity and silence. As an adult I can't imagine beginning my week any other way. When I started identifying myself as a Quaker, a friend asked me if Quakers were like the Amish. Since I knew only a little about Quakers and nothing about the Amish, having never met one, I replied, "Yes, I think they are very similar." In my mind, I hoped we weren't that similar to one another, since I had no desire to live the kind of austere life I believed the Amish lived. Now I know the difference between grim austerity and liberating simplicity, and I realize one can live simply and purposefully with no sense of burden or bondage.

Were we able to roll back time and visit a Friends meetinghouse in the 1800s, we would notice a marked difference in the Quaker attire from that of the general populace. The Quakers' clothing would lack ornamentation or frills; it would be modest in design and restrained in color. The homes to which the Quakers returned would be of simple design, the contents modest, limited to what was needed and little else. They would be free of alcohol, musical instruments, excessive adornment, and worldly entertainment. There would purposefully be little to distract the homes' inhabitants from spiritual contemplation or meaningful labor. Disorder would be frowned upon, as it was considered an indication of a cluttered life and chaotic spirit. There would be, in the words of the proverb, a place for everything and everything in its place.

If we rolled forward to the twenty-first century and entered the doors of a Quaker meetinghouse, we would see it was likely plain, having no stained-glass windows or altar. No statuary would be present, though a Quaker painting might be found, perhaps *Presence in the Midst, None Shall Make Them Afraid,* or one of several versions of Edward Hicks's *The Peaceable Kingdom.* Depending on the meeting and its method of Quaker worship, there may or may not be a piano or organ. Some meetinghouses would have pulpits from which employed pastors would deliver messages; others would lack not only pulpits but also pastors.*

Despite these differences, if you were to ask a modern Quaker what Friends value, it is almost certain the word *simplicity* would

---

* The reasons for those discrepancies are complicated and best understood by reading Wilmer Cooper's *A Living Faith* or Thomas D. Hamm's *The Quakers in America.*

be mentioned before long, if not first. But it is a kind of simplicity clearly different from the simplicity of our spiritual ancestors, having little to do with attire and appearance, and more to do with lifestyle, use of resources, transportation choices, career preferences, and environmental sustainability. Though the expressions of simplicity in ancient and modern times would differ in form, they would be similar in motivation, borne of a conviction that we are called to live a particular way. It is this conviction—our belief in a focused way of life that enables us to pay fuller attention to God, one another, and creation—that draws me

> If you were to ask a modern Quaker what Friends value, it is almost certain the word *simplicity* would be mentioned before long, if not first.

still to Quakerism and its implications for my life. Toward that end, I would like us to think briefly about materialism, simplicity, and our habit of defining our success and happiness by our acquisitions.

The necessity of this recently came to mind when I met a man who had uprooted his family and moved across the country, away from his family, friends, and community, in order to take a job that paid better. Though his previous job had earned him a comfortable lifestyle, his unceasing desire to earn and amass more caused him to surrender the blessings of family and friends for material gain. After the move, his children were miserable, his wife was lonely, and his new work demanded most of his time. The family's new wealth did little to assuage the deep loss of relationship they experienced. Unfortunately, this is being repeated the world over, as more and more people forsake their ties for a perceived, but elusive, gain. It is time we ask ourselves what it means to be successful, consider the true cost of success, and begin to see how our understanding of success cripples our ability to live simply.

What Does It Mean to Be Successful?

In the early years of my time among Friends, I lived down the street from a Quaker woman, Olive Charles, who had moved to our community after teaching at a Friends school in Pennsylvania. Though quite elderly, Olive engaged life fully, devoting most of her working hours to serving others. Fortuitously, a group home for teens with intellectual disabilities had opened next door to her house. Several area residents wanted to bar the home from the neighborhood, fearing it would lower their property values, but Olive was supportive and welcomed the teens the day they arrived. Within a short time, she had organized a Sunday school class for the teens at our Quaker meeting and had persuaded a teacher trained in special education to lead the class. The teens were soon integrated into the life of the meeting, attending nearly every function and making friends with many of its members.

After I moved to the same neighborhood, it became my custom to visit Olive, asking her about Quakerism, which I knew little about. I recall asking her why Quakers used to dress funny. She recalled the plain Friends she had known as a child, then mentioned there were Friends still living, scattered throughout the country in smaller communities, who dressed and spoke in what was called the plain manner. During our visits, I began to notice the simple, almost spare, appearance of her living room. The room was neat and tidy. Each item had a purpose and there were few decorative objects, yet the room had a calming presence about it that was lovely in its own right.

It was during those visits I began to realize how much time we spend accumulating and maintaining things we don't need, and what a distraction they can be, preventing us from focusing on more important matters. I thought of all the people I knew who labored long hours to buy goods—boats, cars, vacations, motor homes, furnishings, clothing, and gadgetry—far beyond their need. I thought of my own circumstances, and how even though I lived alone, my goods had spilled over into a basement and garage and even into a neighboring garage. I thought of the many hours I worked to pay for those items and the time and care I committed to their maintenance. Just the weekend before, I had built shelves in the basement to store future acquisitions.

I also thought of our larger culture and how we measure success by our increase of goods. The area of town where the "successful" people lived boasted disproportionally large homes, furnished to fill even seldom-used rooms. It was my dream to live in such a house one day, and even today, if I am honest, I confess that the urge to acquire has never left me.

Of course, the lifestyle of "never enough" comes with a cost. We exhaust ourselves, working long hours to pay for things we have no time to enjoy. We choose careers based on the income they produce, not on the satisfaction they provide. We assume large amounts of debt that require our continued labor to pay, exhausting ourselves in pursuit of lives that finally hold little pleasure for us. We chain ourselves to devices meant to entertain and connect, yet we find hollowness and isolation instead.

Our quest for more not only depletes our physical resources, it also takes a toll on our relationships, robbing us of the time needed to cultivate and deepen our family ties and friendships. Spouses and partners become estranged, children are left to raise themselves, friendships wither and die. Everything we claim to value—our marriages, our family well-being, our spiritual health, our peace of mind—is put at risk by our headlong pursuit of more. This mad pursuit of more, a quest which is never finished since there is always one new thing to possess, leaves us physically, emotionally, and spiritually spent. We are left unsatisfied, betrayed by the very path we thought would bring meaning and joy, angered by prosperity's failure to keep its promise of happily ever after.

What is needed is a new measure of success, for it is clear the further acquisition of goods is not only unsustainable but also ultimately unsatisfying. Once we have enough—once our physical, emotional, spiritual, and relational needs are met—we must ask ourselves how possessing more things can enrich our lives, given their tendency to finally possess us.

> What is needed is a new measure of success, for it is clear the further acquisition of goods is not only unsustainable but also ultimately unsatisfying.

It is no surprise that in a capitalist culture, the accumulation of wealth would become the standard of success. But there are other facets of our society we also believe are important: civic duty, volunteerism, spirituality, the arts, philanthropy, and education, to name a few. Why hasn't our mastery of those cultural aspects become the commonly accepted standard of success? Why have we granted material wealth such inordinate power to define our success and determine our happiness? Why hasn't the simple contentment of my elderly friend Olive become a goal toward which we aspire?

Simplicity and True Enrichment

I know a family with three grown sons. The oldest is an accomplished musician, plays a number of instruments well, and shares his gift generously and enthusiastically. The middle child is an entrepreneur, has created several businesses, and is now wealthy. The youngest child is the father of two small children and invests his time with them, creating a nurturing home and managing their household while his wife works outside the home. Occasionally I bump into their parents and inquire about their children and grandchildren. Though all their sons are happy, productive, and well situated in life, the parents talk most often about their son in business and his latest triumphs. They seem almost embarrassed by the choices their youngest son has made, assuring me he'll enter the workforce just as soon as his children begin school. As for their oldest son, the musician, they fear he has spent too much time on what should be a hobby and that he will become destitute. I once pointed out that the world needs nurturing fathers and accomplished musicians, and while they quickly agreed, I also sensed no real passion in their affirmation.

We have become so accustomed to defining success in material terms that we have failed to appreciate the other facets of life that enrich and sustain us. Think for a moment of how we venerate material wealth and those who hold it. Why is a person who accumulates pets considered mentally ill, while a person who accumulates money is seen as a role model? The first person is diagnosed with compulsive hoarding syndrome and treated

> Why is a person who accumulates pets considered mentally ill, while a person who accumulates money is seen as a role model?

with therapy and drugs, while the wealthy person is lauded for his or her skills in investing and viewed as a success.

But what if, in determining our success in life, we measured our accomplishments in ways unrelated to possessions and wealth? What if our affirmation of the following questions defined our success?

- Does my work contribute to the well-being of humanity?
- Are my relationships healthy and life affirming?
- Do I connect more with devices or people?
- Am I kind and thoughtful, providing others with helpful emotional support?
- Am I generous, freely sharing with those who have less than I do?
- Do I bring joy and hope to others?
- Am I a thoughtful steward of the resources I oversee?

- Have my actions contributed to peace and understanding?
- Am I careful to protect and nurture the less powerful—children, the disabled, the poor, animals, and nature?
- Have I furthered the advancement of justice in my nation and world?

What if those became the significant questions that defined success? Imagine how our society would improve if the enrichment of others was as important as our own advancement. Simplicity, because it calls us away from rampant self-gratification, makes such an emphasis possible.

Simple Beauty

I once was a guest in the home of a family whose church was sponsoring a workshop I was giving. My hosts were gracious people, making every effort to ensure my brief visit was a pleasant one. While their home was lovely, every available surface was decorated with knickknacks. They were avid collectors, and had clearly been gathering objects for many years. Ironically, on a wall covered with pictures and paintings hung a plaque featuring the word *Simplify*!

I went to sleep thinking about that word and its obvious contradiction with the household around it. I thought of all the winsome words they could have displayed on their wall: *Love,*

Joy, Peace, Family, Friends, Kindness, or *Gratitude.* Instead, they had chosen the word *Simplify.* I considered how often, amidst the clutter and chaos of my own life, when events and circumstances seemed to pile up around me, I had longed for simplicity. Perhaps the word *Simplify* wasn't so much a reflection of my hosts' current priorities as it was their unspoken hope and dream.

The next morning at breakfast, they told me how hectic and complicated their lives were. Though their children were grown and they were both retired, they were busier than ever, indeed overwhelmed.

"We were hoping our lives would become simpler," said the husband. "But that hasn't happened."

Because I was a guest in their home and didn't know them well, I didn't feel comfortable offering them advice, so I just agreed that life could feel overwhelming. But I couldn't help wondering if their outward clutter was symptomatic of an inward chaos, and if the former was alleviated, whether the latter would be remedied. After all, it's no secret that persons wishing to experience clarity and peace often begin by simplifying their surroundings.

My wife and I enjoy visiting the Shaker community at Pleasant Hill, Kentucky. The beauty of the Shaker way is found in the careful arrangement of its buildings upon the land. There is an inherent balance that is not only pleasant to the eye but also soothing to the spirit. This is not accidental; rather, it is a direct consequence of Shaker spirituality, which prizes a purity of line, life, and soul. I have often thought of Shaker design as an American feng shui, an aesthetic that seems to carry with it the power to restore and reorder our minds.

As I acquainted myself with Shaker design, I began to notice how other religious traditions incorporated elements of simplicity into their dwellings and daily routines. I would visit monasteries, retreat centers, and other spaces designed to further our spiritual growth and notice how they were invariably basic. Furnishings were prized for their usefulness, not their expense. Food was appreciated for its nutritional value, and clothing for its durability and service. Entertainment was almost always communal in nature, involving and engaging others, seldom a solitary pursuit.

That morning, over breakfast with the retired couple, I told them about a Shaker community within driving distance of their home and urged them to visit it when they had time, which they eventually did. The visit was transformative. They returned home, took stock of their surroundings, donated many of their goods to Goodwill, and divested themselves of the trappings that required constant maintenance and care. I later learned they had even sold their large home and moved to a smaller residence. I don't believe one visit to a Shaker community brought about this dramatic change, but I do think it confirmed what had become a growing desire on their part: to live a liberated life, freed from multiple distractions. I suspect the word *Simplify* on their wall was their initial movement toward a more meaningful life.

Simplicity Is Gradual

When my wife and I were young, we thought success was measured by the accumulation of goods and wealth. We committed much time and effort toward that goal, only to reach it and discover we didn't feel successful. Instead, we felt stressed and tired, and eventually disenchanted and disappointed. Some of us didn't like the persons we had become, feeling grasping and self-absorbed. When the essayist Anna Quindlen quoted a postcard she'd received, "If you win the rat race, you're still just a rat," we knew what she meant.

Aware of our unhappiness, we envied those persons whose lives were marked with a serenity lacking in ours. Eventually, we realized our definition of success needed to change, and we were inspired to make different choices. We wished we had arrived at this understanding earlier and regretted time lost with our family or spent in jobs we didn't find fulfilling. But those were necessary steps on our way toward a more meaningful life, helping teach us the true meaning of success. Determined not to let our children single-mindedly chase after material riches, we taught them the importance of family, of love, of leisure, of togetherness, of friendships, of helping the neighbor, and of giving back to the community. But this is a lesson each of us must learn for ourselves. No amount of urging and coercion can make us reorder our priorities. Life, not lectures, inspires us to change.

Just as we cannot compel someone else to live simply, we

cannot define simplicity for another, for our needs vary, as does our capacity for change. The life of simplicity is one of growing awareness, and each of us grows at different rates, in diverse ways. Not many decades had passed before early Quakers began judging one another's commitment to simplicity, gauging another's devotion to God by his or her clothing, home, and speech. They then enacted strict rules governing simplicity. It ended disastrously, creating a climate of judgment and self-righteousness that caused grave injury to our spiritual well-being.

In my early twenties when I began thinking seriously about simplicity, I had friends who drove a luxurious car. To be fair, I

> We cannot define simplicity for another, for our needs vary, as does our capacity for change.

drove a Volkswagen Beetle, so every car seemed luxurious in comparison. Whenever I saw my friends, I wondered why they didn't drive a simple, more affordable vehicle. I wanted them to conform to my understanding of simplicity. What I didn't know is that the woman had suffered a back injury years before that had made travel very painful; hence their decision to own a larger, more comfortable car. Not understanding that, I found myself judging them.

Simplicity is not a universal fit. What is extravagance to one is necessity for another. My interpretation of wants and needs will not be yours, nor will yours be mine. The life of simplicity does not mean owning a bare minimum of goods. It is a commitment to live a liberated life, freed from constant distraction, devoted to our spiritual and emotional growth and the betterment of others. This can, and will, take many forms, depending upon our priorities, insights, needs, and life stages. Our needs in our child-rearing years are different from the needs of our retirement years. While our journey toward a simpler life might well take different roads, it begins with the same step—the discernment between *wants* and *needs*.

Wanting and Needing

There are, the saying goes, two ways to be rich: one is to make more, the other is to want less. Most of us, when given that choice, have opted to make more. The idea of doing without, of denying

> There are two ways to be rich: one is to make more, the other is to want less. Most of us, when given that choice, have opted to make more.

ourselves the things we want, seems almost unfair. Advertisers tell us we "deserve" to drive a new car or "need" a larger television. It is easy to convince ourselves we merit these things, especially since we have worked so hard. But it is a vicious cycle, for we have worked much in order to buy the things we believe we need, often without stopping to consider whether they are essential.

I once received a phone call from a distraught woman, short on funds, asking for a loan to tide her over. She had two bills to pay, a cable television bill and a water bill, and she couldn't decide which one she should pay. Her monthly cable bill exceeded one hundred dollars. I pointed out that cable TV was not a necessity, that she wasn't homebound, that there were other ways to entertain herself, that many people lived happy, productive lives without television, but that water was a necessity. I urged her to drop cable TV. I told her many people were quite happy without television. But in her mind she was unable to move cable TV from her *needs* list to her *wants* list. Television had become a necessity, as important as water.

She is not alone. Pay attention and notice how naturally we use the words *want* and *need* interchangeably, as if they were synonymous. Not long ago, I visited a bakery, where I told the young lady working the counter that I *needed* a donut. As I waited for my donut, I heard others use the language of need when ordering their pastries. It occurred to me that none of us *needed* the things we'd ordered. Our use of the word *need* seems to have grown exponentially. This is no small matter, for it creates in our minds an urgency to acquire, a compulsion to purchase and consume more and more.

I recently mentioned to my wife that we *needed* a new car, pointing out that our car was nearly seven years old and had over 120,000 miles on it. "I don't think it's going to last much longer," I said.

"Really?" she said. "It seems to be running perfectly fine."

Some friends had purchased a new car not long before; I had been impressed with its features and had been thinking of little else since. I explained how buying a new car would actually save us money in the long run, an argument we both knew to be untrue—for it is, except in rare instances, always less expensive to keep the car you have. I finally admitted I had envied our friends' car. My wife suggested it would be more practical to clean our old car, which we did, vacuuming, cleaning, and waxing the vehicle until it shone. Because she is a kind person, she didn't point out that I had confused what I *wanted* with what I *needed*.

The distinction between *want* and *need* was much clearer to earlier generations, raised during the Great Depression. As we struggle through our global recession today, it might well become a necessary distinction again, requiring us to live more simply whether we wish to or not. This newfound frugality needn't be a development to fear. In learning the differences between our wants and needs we might discover our lives have also become less complicated and stressful. It is no coincidence that when our grandparents recall the Great Depression, they speak not only of the hardships, which were very real for many people, but also, almost longingly, of the ways in which people shared with one another.

While I don't wish to romanticize financial hardship, knowing it can exact a terrible toll, it can also help us develop the virtues of interdependence, generosity, simplicity, and gratitude.

> It could well be that simplicity, not materialism, is the avenue to a new American Dream.

Indeed, the virtues we learn in times of scarcity might well be the tools that provide an economic lift to our culture. As generosity displaces greed and interdependence replaces self-interest, we will begin to create a society that blesses everyone, not just a wealthy minority. It could well be that simplicity, not materialism, is the avenue to a new American Dream.

Hallmarks of the Simple Life

At the heart of simplicity are found several essential values: awareness, generosity, patience, persistence, and focus. No consideration of simplicity is complete without dwelling on these principles and their connection to the simple life.

Awareness

While a *want* for one person might be a *need* for another, the criteria for defining wants and needs will be similar. The first step in understanding the difference is *awareness.* Do we acquire material goods impulsively, or do we give careful thought to our purchases? While we tend to be more deliberate about buying costly items like cars and homes, it is also wise to reflect for a moment before purchasing less expensive items, if only to cultivate the habit of thoughtfulness. The delay associated with reflection permits us to catch our breath and check our impulse to acquire.

When my wife and I first began using a credit card, we quickly became accustomed to the ease of purchasing. Before, we had to consult our checkbook or billfold to see if we had sufficient funds, weighing whether or not we could afford a particular item. But the availability of credit eliminated that pause and we soon found ourselves purchasing things without thought, seldom stopping to discern whether we actually needed them. In the past, we would ask ourselves, *Can we make do without this? Do we have something else that can serve the same purpose? If we buy this today, will we have money to pay that bill tomorrow? Will this make us happy or improve our lives? Are there hidden costs associated with this? Will we have to maintain it or insure it or store it?* With significant credit at our disposal, those questions were no longer asked. It was enough simply to want it. Within a short time, the items we purchased began to feel like necessities and it became difficult to deny ourselves these goods.

We would later read that people who use credit spend up to 20 percent more than people who use cash. The physical act of having to count our money to determine whether something can be afforded is a powerful deterrent to excessive spending. It introduces the element of *awareness,* which is critical in the life of simplicity. While my wife and I still use a credit card, it is now our custom to pay our credit card debt in its entirety each month, be acutely aware of how much credit we've used, and to delay or deny ourselves the purchase of noncritical items. We have discovered debit cards are even more helpful since they do not allow us to spend beyond the amount in our checking account. Of course, we are not perfect and sometimes neglect these habits and have to relearn them. The discernment between *wants* and *needs* is the work of a lifetime, as we grow in understanding and sensitivity to our needs and the needs of the world.

Awareness is not only a personal issue but also a communal one. So we ask ourselves, before making a purchase, how the things we buy and use affect others, and whether they are a product of human and animal suffering. When new clothing is purchased at rock-bottom prices, somewhere in the world a laborer is being exploited. That laborer might be a child in a developing nation, a destitute woman in India, or a prisoner in China. The food we eat, especially food that is animal-based, is often the product of inhumane treatment. *Awareness* means far more than discerning between our wants and needs; it means giving careful consideration to how our needs are met and their cost to other living beings.

The Quaker John Woolman, born in 1720 in New Jersey, embodied the virtues of simplicity and awareness. Enjoying early success in business, he soon realized his work demanded too much of his time, precluding the work of justice to which he felt called. He then became a tailor and orchardist, taking care to leave ample time for ministry.

Woolman was committed to ending slavery, so he traveled from one Quaker community to another, urging Friends who had not yet rejected the practice of slavery to free their slaves and pay them a fair wage. He refused to personally benefit from slave labor, paying slaves for any work done on his behalf. Learning that the dyes using in clothing were injurious to the workers in the dye industry, he wore only undyed clothing. Concerned about the use of slave labor to mine silver, he declined to use silver dining implements. Woolman walked instead of riding stagecoaches, troubled by the abuse of horses that were worked to the point of exhaustion. In all these ways and more, Woolman demonstrated a keen awareness of how others had been exploited in the processes of production. Because of his witness, slavery became discouraged among Friends, and by 1784 one could not be a Quaker in good standing and be a slaveholder.

This careful thought, this awareness, becomes second nature

to those committed to the life of simplicity. But it is not a burdensome effort, sucking the joy out of life. Rather, awareness becomes a spiritual exercise that breathes creativity and energy into our lives. As we differentiate between our wants and needs and become more aware of the true cost of things, we feel energized and experience a serenity we had not yet known. We feel more in control of our lives and begin to realize how our possessions enslave us, limiting our options and choices in life because of the demands they place on us and the resources and support

> Awareness becomes a spiritual exercise that breathes creativity and energy into our lives.

they require. We recognize our material goods exact a cost beyond their initial purchase—complicating our lives, squandering scarce resources, harming others, and fueling our desire to possess even more. John Woolman believed the root of war began in our quest for more. "May we look upon our treasures, and the furniture of our Houses, and our Garments in which we array ourselves, and [discern] whether the seeds of war have any nourishment in these our possessions, or not."*

---

* John Woolman, "A Plea for the Poor," quoted in *John Woolman: The Journal and Major Essays,* ed. Amelia Mott Gummere (New York: Macmillan, 1922), 419.

Today, we are acutely aware that our demand for oil has fueled inequity and violence around the globe. As people in developing nations desire the same lifestyle we enjoy, even more aggression might result as we contend for limited resources. But one needn't look around the globe to see the pitfalls of unbridled consumption. We surround ourselves with the latest technological marvels, having been told they will simplify our lives, only to discover they exact a great cost in stress, time, and money. We spend much time yoked to the very devices we hoped would liberate us. This is being repeated the world over. Our failure to live simply might well be the world's, and our personal, undoing.

Generosity

While cultivating awareness helps us discern our wants from our needs, we still find ourselves burdened with far more than we need. I had a friend who began to appreciate the value of simplicity. Addicted to electronic gadgetry, he vowed to stop chasing after the latest products. This did nothing to solve his current dilemma: a house filled to the brim with items he neither needed nor appreciated. He had seven televisions—one in each bedroom, the kitchen, the living room, his home office, and basement. He held a yard sale, sold those and many other items he no longer needed, and gave the money to a local charity, experiencing more satisfaction in that one act of giving than in his many acquisitions.

When our children were young, my wife and I purchased a new pop-up camper. We enjoyed it for eight years, until our children's schedules made family vacations rarer and more difficult. The camper sat unused for a year, though still requiring insurance, licensing, upkeep, winterizing, and storage. While my wife and I were dining with friends, they mentioned their desire to purchase a camper. The parents of young children, they envisioned several years of vacation fun while their children were still little. Impulsively, my wife and I said, "Please take our camper." They refused, believing it too extravagant a gift to accept. We persisted, explaining that we had gotten a great deal of enjoyment from it, that it had not been used in over a year, that it bothered us to see it sitting unused, that it had served our purposes well when our children were younger, but no longer did. They relented and accepted it as a gift, promising to share it with others as we had shared it with them. We signed the title over to them, and they have used it many times since, with much enjoyment. When they no longer use it, they will pass it on to someone else, multiplying the satisfaction they drew from it.

When my wife and I were first married, we would speculate about the things we could do if we won the lottery. That was unlikely to happen since we didn't play the lottery, but that did not prevent us from dreaming aloud what we would do with the money. We talked about how fun it would be to share our wealth with others, improving their lives. Eventually, it occurred to us that if we lived beneath our means, if we spent less than we earned, we would in effect win the lottery and be able to share with others. It also occurred to us that most people who needed help didn't need tens of thousands of dollars. Some were in between jobs and needed their mortgage paid for a month or two. Others had unanticipated automotive or medical expenses. They did not require the assistance of someone with great wealth. They needed a friend with sufficient resources to provide for their own modest needs, one who would also be willing to assist others with their needs. Philanthropy and generosity are not the purview of the wealthy. Even the poorest among us are given opportunities to be generous.

When our children were born, a woman in our Quaker meeting simplified her schedule to make herself available as a baby-sitter several days a week. It was her gift to us, caring for our small sons in the parsonage where we lived. The value of her gift was immense, leading to a deep friendship which continues to this day. She now resides in a nursing home, and so now it is our turn to simplify our schedule to spend time with her.

Our commitment to simplicity is often the start of a new life of generosity. We become aware of the resources available to us—more resources than we need to live happy, fulfilling lives—and we begin to notice opportunities to enhance and expand the lives of others. One couple in my Quaker meeting are retired educators. Learning about a public school in the Deep South that lacked even paper and pencils, they began soliciting school supplies from their network of friends. What they couldn't collect, they purchased themselves, then transported the supplies hundreds of miles to the impoverished students. They do this every year. Had they spent their retirement indulging themselves, spending time and money on their own comforts, they would not have been in a position to generously assist others.

Where generosity is missing, simplicity descends into a miserliness of spirit; we live modestly, but only to amass money. Generosity calls us beyond self-absorption, allowing us to enrich the world with our time, skill, and material blessings. Generosity is a corrective, guarding against our tendency to hoard. It opens our eyes, permitting us to see the needs of others. As we become aware of the good our generosity can accomplish, simplicity becomes a joy, not a burden. We strive to live modestly, so that more and more of our resources are available to others. This

> As we become aware of the good our generosity can accomplish, simplicity becomes a joy, not a burden.

doesn't mean we never treat ourselves; a delicious meal at a fine restaurant, a concert, a vacation to a lovely, restful place can still be enjoyed. But against the backdrop of simplicity, these extravagances will be appreciated all the more for their relative rarity.

Generosity gives us the life we dreamed of when we were pursuing material gain. We find, in acts of generosity, the joy that had eluded us. But more than that, we discover this was the reason we were created—to give and share with others. We discover our generosity is repaid in kind, that as we share with others, blessings find us out—peace of mind, serenity, sufficiency, beauty, and contentment. I am not speaking of the financial prosperity we are promised by televangelists when we donate to their cause. That is a manipulation of the worst sort, exploiting the naive for selfish gain. I am saying that generosity begets generosity, just as violence begets violence, and that an orientation of generosity toward the world creates in turn a global graciousness, from which all benefit.

Patience and Persistence

For the first fourteen years of our marriage, my wife and I lived in rental properties and housing paid for by the Quaker meetings I pastored. When, in our late thirties, we decided to buy our first home, we hired a Realtor who asked to know our annual income so she could gauge what kind of house we could afford. We had no other debt, and she cheerfully informed us we could afford a large beautiful home. This excited me, since I had always wanted a large, beautiful home. But my wife urged us to live beneath our means and purchase a more modest home, which we did.

We have lived in our home for over a dozen years, but I still catch myself thinking how nice it would be to have a larger home. I've wondered how long it will be before I no longer entertain such thoughts, and I have concluded that this might be a lifelong struggle for me. Perhaps it is difficult for you too. Most of us have lived all our lives in a materialistic culture that judges our success and happiness by our possessions. The habit of acquisition is deeply ingrained in us, despite our best intentions to live beneath our means. Compounding our difficulty is the constant bombardment we experience from television, advertisements, friends, and neighbors to amass even more belongings, many of them not only unnecessary but also real barriers to our liberation and joy. Indeed, society's encouragement to buy and acquire is so relentless we never really escape it. Even if we are able to slip away to a quiet place, we catch ourselves, in stray moments, thinking of the next thing we want to own. We grow discouraged, believing a life of simplicity is not possible unless we move to the country and join the Amish.

We forget that acquisition is learned behavior, cultivated over many years, the embers of materialism stoked to a roaring blaze. The fire will not be doused overnight. Just as the flames are extinguished in one area of our lives, sparks will ignite the dry tinder in another spot and we will find ourselves once again ablaze with desire for more.

Several years ago, our home was struck by lightning, causing a small section of our roof to burn. The firefighters arrived quickly, dousing the fire with extinguishers. They lingered long after the initial fire, knowing the tendency of dormant fire to spring to life again. (Fortunately, this time, it didn't.)

But so it is with us and the simple life; just when we believe we have quenched our hunger for more, the desire roars back, consuming us.

This is why the life of simplicity requires patience and persistence. The fires of desire spring to life again, and we catch ourselves falling back into the familiar patterns of acquisition. Having slipped, we condemn ourselves for our weakness. But recriminations are seldom helpful. Instead, we learn from our missteps and then establish patterns of living to lessen temptation. Recovering alcoholics discover it isn't wise to frequent bars. Those committed to simplicity learn to avoid the places and situations that trigger the impulse to buy and accumulate. A friend of mine, when she committed to a life of simplicity, soon realized she could no longer visit shopping malls and peruse catalogs or Internet shopping sites, lest she be lured back into a lifestyle she no longer wanted. She began spending her spare time reading, sharing meals with friends, and writing letters of loving support to persons undergoing difficulty, activities she found far more satisfying than shopping.

Acquisition is addictive. We experience a high when we enter a store and see the things we want on sale. Merchandisers know this, which is why the first word we usually see when we enter a store is the word *Sale!* We read that word and are energized and excited, hurrying to the racks and shelves to scan the bargains. But like all addictions, our obsession to possess can be overcome. It will not be easy. Anyone who has ever conquered a deep craving knows discipline and persistence are required, and that even when we think we have our compulsion mastered, it slips into our lives again.

A woman I know struggles with alcoholism. When she agreed to seek counseling, I was elated, believing it signaled the end of her addiction. She remained sober for three months before drinking again. In a conversation with an addictions counselor, I learned relapse was common and that many alcoholics are never able to break the grip of alcohol on their lives. Addictions of any sort, be they emotional, material, or physical, are never easily shed. Though we hear of people who've experienced seemingly miraculous delivery from an addiction, we forget their liberation was often preceded by years of struggle. This will be no less true with our efforts to live simply. Our habit of acquisition was years in the making and might take as many years to break. But we need not view ourselves as failures when we stumble. We can remind ourselves of the value of persistence and begin again, with a renewed commitment to the simple life, a bit wiser, a bit more aware of the events that might trigger our relapse.

Persistence is especially important because not everyone will be pleased with our changed priorities. Some will interpret it as a judgment of their own choices and will urge us to adopt a way of life similar to their own. This road, of course, runs both ways. We will do the same thing to them, believing when others choose our lifestyle it confirms the decisions we've made. Just as we should not abandon our commitment to simplicity in the face of criticism, neither should we disparage those who've chosen differently, for there are few things as annoying as a true believer bent on making others see the light.

We should be patient with others, trusting that if the Spirit calls them to a life of simplicity, the Spirit is quite capable of guiding them into that life as they are ready.

We should be persistent with ourselves, not growing discouraged by our missteps and giving up, but committing ourselves anew, with faith and good cheer, to the rich life of simplicity.

Focus

We have considered so far the values of awareness, generosity, patience, and persistence, and their relationship to the simple life. Now I would like for us to think about the importance of focus. I wrote above of John Woolman and how success in his vocation distracted him from the life of justice to which he felt called. This desire for focus is a common theme in the simple life. We begin to realize how our many commitments, even those obligations we consider good and helpful, cause us to become distracted and lose sight of our priorities, ultimately impairing our commitment to a meaningful life. We become preoccupied by peripheral issues, our gaze is no longer directed forward, and we lose our way.

When I was a child, a man in our town had a horse and carriage he rode on Saturday mornings. One summer morning he came past our house, asking my brothers and me if we wanted a ride. We quickly agreed and climbed into the carriage. We noticed the horse was fitted with a device that blocked its side vision. When we asked the man what it was, he said it was a pair of blinders, and explained they kept the horse from being startled or distracted by peripheral activity, allowing it to stay focused on its forward path.

At the time it seemed cruel to not permit the animal full visual range, though now I have come to appreciate the benefits of focused attention, especially as I observe the pervasive distractions in our culture. We are bombarded with noise, text messages, phone calls, advertisements, music, and commercials intended to draw our attention toward a product, person, or service. There is no escaping this visual and auditory barrage. It begins early in the day when alarm radios blast us out of bed and is a constant companion through the day until we fall into bed, jangled and exhausted. The possibility for sustained and focused thought is compromised nearly every waking moment. We are distracted beings in an agitated world.

My wife and I own a farmhouse on land that has been in her family for six generations. (It seems wrong for a man who cherishes simplicity to own a second home, but such is the trap of sentimentality.) The farmhouse is isolated, the nearest town, a rather small one, is a dozen miles away, cell phone coverage is spotty, and we've never installed a telephone or television. Much of our time there is spent reading, hiking in the woods that surround the farmhouse, or tending to the home and flower gardens. Occasionally, the neighbor who lives a half mile down the road will stop by to visit. Otherwise, days can pass without our visiting or talking with anyone outside the family.

This way of life was typical for our ancestors, who were undistracted by telephone and television, not to mention smartphones, iPads, and every manner of digital device. Though their work was demanding, it was balanced by Sabbath rest, family togetherness, and a social schedule that didn't consume their every waking moment. I catch a glimpse of this life when we visit our farmhouse and enjoy its unhurried pace. We take pleasure in lingering conversations on the porches, uninterrupted by ringing telephones. Board games take the place of video games and television, and home-cooked meals replace fast food. Many of the diversions of modern life are dispensed with, as if blinders have been used to better focus our attention. I am sometimes reluctant to return to our regular lives, which are too often filled with the clamor so common in contemporary times.

But I have discovered it is possible to re-create the pastoral peace of our rural life, even amidst the press of our many commitments. It begins with the recognition that the many devices we own are our servants, not our rulers. Phones do not have to be answered, texts and e-mails do not have to be instantly acknowledged, nor does every request for our time have to be granted. Television programs do not have to be watched. Children do not have to play in multiple sports or participate in every school event, requiring our evenings and weekends. The peripheral events not central to our lives can be dispensed with, permitting us to center on more meaningful aspects of life.

This is not to say the simple life is one of grim austerity. In fact, just the opposite is true. In concentrating on what is most important, we discover an abundance we had not known. Our

> In concentrating on what is most important, we discover an abundance we had not known.

family relationships are deepened, our friendships are cultivated, our minds and spirits are enlivened, our mental and physical health are improved as our lives become less stressful. The proper focusing of our time and resources is the first step toward a new and better life.

In the name of advancement and progress, we have created a world increasingly difficult to inhabit. Our opportunities for rest and renewal are fewer and fewer; inventions designed to save time, money, and effort have complicated life to an extent we never imagined. In my own household, five telephones have taken the place of one. Four of those telephones are portable, following my family and me wherever we go, pulling us away from conversations, rest, and needed solitude. In addition to ringing incessantly, they regularly present texts demanding responses. The computer I purchased to simplify my life delivers fifty e-mails a day, only a handful of them necessary, but each of them requiring my time and attention. Never in the history of the world has communication been so easy and simultaneously so distracting and pointless.

Assailed by these and other demands, we find it nearly impossible to still our minds. We feel anxious and strained, wishing life wasn't so complicated. When we do have time to imagine and reflect, we catch ourselves thinking of those places and times when life was more simple and serene. We wonder how our lives became marked with such intensity, and wonder whether the choices we've made can be reconsidered in light of their toll on us. This is the beginning of intentional living, our dawning realization that life can be simpler, less cluttered with demands and obligations we find increasingly meaningless.

Achieving the Simple Life

If awareness, generosity, patience, persistence, and focus are the hallmarks of the simple life, how do we incorporate these qualities into our lives? How do we discern when they might be particularly helpful, especially if they have not been intentional priorities for us in the past?

Silence and Centering as the Gateway
to the Simple Life

When I first became a Quaker, it was in a Friends meeting that employed a pastor who delivered weekly messages. For several years, I wasn't aware there were other Quakers who met in silence, so when I was first exposed to that manner of worship in my early twenties, I was not only surprised but somewhat anxious at the thought of sitting in silence for an hour waiting for the Spirit to inspire someone to talk. Eventually, a woman did rise to speak about a challenge she had faced and how God had given her insight about how best to meet it. She urged us to trust in the Spirit's ability to guide our daily lives. Though her counsel was helpful, the hour passed interminably slowly, and I left the meetinghouse vowing never to let myself get trapped in such a setting again.

Despite my vow, I soon found myself back in silent worship after agreeing to take members of a college class I attended to an unprogrammed Quaker meeting.* Again, the hour passed slowly and I found myself worrying my fellow students would think Quakers odd for practicing what seemed to me to be a bizarre form of worship. To my surprise, they not only tolerated the meeting for worship, they enjoyed it, discussing at length how refreshing the silence had been. Our professor, a man I greatly admired,

---

* Quaker meetings that employ a pastor are typically referred to as programmed meetings. Those meetings that don't employ pastors and that worship on the basis of silence are called unprogrammed meetings.

was especially profuse in his praise and made plans to return again. It was then I began to think I had misjudged the value of silence, and decided to incorporate silent centering into my life.

It didn't take me long to discover that sitting quietly in a room wasn't helpful. My mind would drift, or I would grow sleepy. I knew others who spent an hour each day in silence, but I didn't seem able to sit quietly for even ten minutes. Discouraged, I mentioned this problem to a friend who laughed and said, "Of course, you can't sit quietly. You're hyper. You're always in motion. You need to figure out another way to be silent."

Shortly afterward, I read about a man who practiced Buddhist walking meditation. The article didn't describe this devotional practice, and Google hadn't yet been invented for me to look it up and learn more. Though I wasn't Buddhist, I was open to the idea the Buddhists might have something to teach me and thought if the Buddhists had found it helpful to meditate while walking, I could too. I ended that day with a two-mile walk around my neighborhood. It was a positive experience, so I repeated it the next day and the day after that until it became a habit. I returned from each walk physically refreshed and spiritually focused.

After we moved to our current home, I began walking in the woods near our house. I was often the only one in those woods, so I felt comfortable folding my hands in a posture of prayer as I walked. This simple practice seemed to focus my attention even more sharply. Sometimes I would stop, sit on a bench, and reflect on the view around me—the stream, the tall trees, the birds flitting from bush to bush, enjoying the pace and rhythm of nature. Time and again, I would enter the woods weighed down with a problem, only to walk out an hour later with a fresh insight and clarity of mind, sensing a positive way forward. Meditative walking permitted a concentration of thought and power simply not possible in my otherwise distracted life.

As I was describing this practice to a fellow Quaker, she brightened and offered, "That's exactly what I experience in silent worship when I center down." I had heard other Quakers use the term *centering down,* and I had used it myself, inviting Friends to center down at the opening of our meeting for worship. I had initially understood *centering down* as Quaker code words for "It's time to be quiet." But over time those words came to mean much more. I discovered in that practice a careful peeling away of the nonessential to reveal the core of life, the essence of Being. Just as many possessions complicated my efforts toward simplicity, so too did my many mental distractions. In centering down, I laid those preoccupations aside, paring life down to its simplest form.

But true centering down transcends worship. It is to bring one's entire life into a place of listening and learning. Receptivity to the Divine Presence is so much more than an activity undertaken on Sunday morning; rather, it becomes the pattern for all of life, so that every aspect of our lives is held to the Light, fearlessly examined, and stripped to its essence.

It would be impossible for me to overemphasize the importance of the focused life. For when life is not centered, we fall prey to the distractions of self-absorption, materialism, and shallow living. Every dimension of life—our relationships, our worship, our vocations—is only a veneer, when depth is most needed. This centered life begins with our commitment to strip away the unessential and get to the heart.

When I was a child, my grandfather gave me a wooden cage with a ball inside. There was no door on the cage, and the ball was considerably larger than any opening in the bars. It took me a

> When life is not centered, we fall prey
> to the distractions of self-absorption,
> materialism, and shallow living.

while to figure out how the ball got in there. It had been carved from a single block of wood—the extraneous wood whittled away until only the cage and ball remained. These many years later, the sculpture sits in my office, reminding me to discern the essential from the nonessential, retaining the former while whittling away the latter. I need to be reminded of this, for my tendency is usually the opposite, to add the unnecessary to my life until I have lost sight of the Center. Fortunately, the opposite is also true: when I am focused on the Center of life, each segment of my life has the potential to be transformed and made whole and well.

Simplicity Involves One's Whole Being

Simplicity involves the whole of one's being—the spiritual, the physical, the psychological, the emotional, the material, the relational, and the vocational. We no sooner simplify one area of our lives than we sense the need for simplicity in other areas of our lives. Initially, I found the simplicity of Quaker worship unsettling, but in time I came to appreciate it. As my understanding of simplicity grew, and my appreciation for it deepened, I began to wonder how it could inform the entirety of my life. Because I didn't earn much money, it made sense to apply the practice of simplicity to my standard of living. I selected as my teachers persons whose simple lifestyles enabled them to give generously to those in need. Fortunately, I had attached myself to a community of faith in which many had made that choice; these individuals were happy to educate and assist me as I embarked upon that same life.

Within a short time, I began to reflect more deeply upon my vocation and its role in my life and our world. My job at the time left me unsatisfied, and I began to experience the tug toward the pastoral ministry. I saw in that vocation the opportunity to shape thought, influence society in a positive manner, and create the kind of spiritual community that embodied grace, compassion, and generosity.

Around that same time, I met my wife and was taken with her practicality, intelligence, and kindness (not to mention her beauty). She had a growing appreciation for simplicity, an eagerness to help others, and little interest in materialism. Yet another aspect of my life became informed and influenced by my growing appreciation of simplicity and those who practiced it.

All of these experiences have led me to conclude that simplicity is a journey; each year, each experience, each encounter is instructive. I learn from my successes in simplicity—and also from my failures. What I hope for is the permeation of

> This is the key to true wealth: learning not only to live with less but also learning to *want* less.

simplicity across the breadth of my life. While I haven't successfully incorporated simplicity into every aspect of life, I do know this: I am most joyful when I am living as deeply in the way of thoughtful simplicity as I am able. Modest living can be meaningful living.

A Quaker woman I knew possessed significant wealth throughout most of her adult life. Due to a variety of factors, her finances declined in her senior years, and she began living more modestly. Rather than resenting the circumstances that had led to her economic downturn, she experienced a freedom she had never felt before. Near the end of her life, she said, "I am so grateful for all the things I no longer want."

This is the key to true wealth: not only learning to live with less but also learning to *want* less. When that happens, our energies are directed away from acquisition and consumption, toward spiritual, emotional, psychological, and relational growth. At life's end, we will push back from the table, full and satisfied. A banquet was spread before us, and we partook of the most substantive fare life had to offer: love, joy, compassion, community, generosity, and more. This is the abundant life of which Jesus spoke—and not only Jesus but also other great teachers that God has given our world. Collectively, they teach us that outward treasures have no inward profit, and that those lives that are arrayed against the plainest velvet, like precious gems, will possess the greatest beauty.

Peace

When I was a child, I witnessed a fight on the school playground after school. Two older boys squared off, one a bully and the other his victim. That day, the long-suffering victim decided he'd had enough, and after the two circled each other for a while, he punched his tormentor solidly in the nose. Contrary to the conventional myth of bullies being cowards at heart, the bully did not slink off, his tail between his legs. Instead, he attacked the other boy with a vengeance, striking him in the face and stomach. The other boy fought back, kicking and hitting, until both boys were bloodied. The violence nauseated and frightened me.

Over forty years later, I can recall that brutal schoolyard scene with perfect clarity, and I still feel the same sense of revulsion I felt then. My feelings about violence have not changed; the sight of one human inflicting pain upon another disgusts me, whether the pain is physical or mental. Even today, I cannot watch boxing without being repulsed. Can you imagine any sport as cruelly sadistic as when one man attempts to batter the other into unconsciousness, spurred on by a cheering throng of people who will applaud as a fellow human is beaten so severely he suffers a concussion and loss of consciousness? Glee at the suffering of another is surely symptomatic of a troubled spirit.

The bully on the playground remained in our town. In the ensuing years, I would witness his descent into a morass of wanton cruelty. It isn't uncommon to hear people dismiss bullying as a phase persons will grow out of as they mature, but I have seldom seen that happen. What I have observed, in my work as a pastor, is the bully's tendency to grow into even more aberrant behavior—self-loathing, spousal and child abuse, criminality, self-harm, drug or alcohol abuse—leading inevitably to estrangement from family and the human community. Perhaps the horror I felt that long-ago day arose from my sense that two humans were being damaged, and not just those two but also all who witnessed that hostility.

I have known some bullies who were healed by religion, but I have known others who use religion to harass and intimidate others, doing violence in the name of God. I have seen bullies mask their violence in the guise of patriotism, hurting and killing while professing their love for country. But brutality on behalf of God and country is still brutality, and though it has been made to seem virtuous, it is as morally repugnant as violence born of self-interest.

The mental, moral, and spiritual deficiencies that plague the bully can also afflict entire groups, tribes, and nations, until they too consider violence to be a virtue.* When thirty-seven cents of every United States tax dollar is spent on past and current warfare, while only two cents of every tax dollar is spent on diplomacy, international assistance, and war prevention, one could reasonably conclude the United States is suffering from a collective psychosis.† The symptoms of our psychosis are obvious: military spending far outpaces any other expenditure in our federal budget; our movies, television shows, and video games are sadistically vicious; our sports are increasingly aggressive; our murder rate far outpaces the homicide rates of most other nations. In 2010, the Iraqi Body Count Project tallied 4,045 *civilian* murders. During that same year in the United States, there were 14,748 homicide victims, according to the FBI. Ironically, that figure was the lowest number of murders since 1969, so was heralded as an advance against violent crime. Think about that—10,703 more civilians were murdered in the United States than in Iraq, a nation in which a war targeting civilians was

---

* By *spiritual,* I mean not only one's orientation to a Divine Being but also one's recognition of and appreciation for the inherent worth of their fellow humans.

† Friends Committee on National Legislation, "Where Do Our Income Tax Dollars Go," http://fcnl.org/assets/flyer/FCNL_Taxes12.pdf. For further information on war spending, you can visit their website at FCNL.org.

being waged, and we celebrated because it was the lowest murder rate in our nation in forty-one years! At our murderous peak, in 1991, we slew 24,703 of our fellow citizens. There is no escaping the fact that hostility has become a national pastime.

Though we moderns have raised violence to an art form, it is not a phenomenon unique to our culture. Its presence is rife in the sacred scriptures of almost every religion. It has plagued every century, and almost every nation, culture, and political movement. Violence is so pervasive it has been present even in those movements that have sought to eradicate it. For the seeds of violence are rooted in our desire to change and manipulate another, inevitably through coercion, which first violates the will and spirit of another, then does violence to his or her body.

I wish I could say Quakers have been exempt from the temptation of violence, but we owe our religious existence to its presence and have engaged in it ourselves, if not physically, then spiritually and emotionally. While a popular perception of Quakers is our commitment to peace, the first Quakers, as I describe below, were no strangers to violence, and even today Friends participate in war at a level unthinkable a hundred years ago. There are varying reasons for this, chief among them humanity's tendency to believe certain types of aggression will end all violence, which is magical thinking and has never proven to be the case.

In his lecture *Militant Seedbeds of Early Quakerism,* the British historian and Quaker David Boulton observed that the earliest Quakers were ardent supporters of Oliver Cromwell, serving as soldiers in Cromwell's New Model Army. In 1658, George Fox wrote Cromwell a letter chastising him for not attacking Holland, Spain, Turkey, and the Vatican. "Let thy soldiers go forth…that thou may rock nations as a cradle!" wrote Fox. In his pamphlet *To the Council of Officers of the Armie,* Fox urged the troops to "see that you know a soldier's place…and that ye be soldiers qualified." He then observed that one Quaker soldier was worth seven non-Quakers.

It was only when Oliver Cromwell was overthrown and the king restored to power that George Fox and early Friends embraced pacifism. Some have speculated the Quaker movement toward pacifism was self-serving, intended only to show the king they no longer posed a military threat. Others believe that only after aligning themselves with violence did Quakers grow convinced of the futility of violence and its inability to bring about significant and positive change. Whichever the case, early Friends' alliance with the army was soon abandoned and quickly written out of our popular history.*

But when we forget our history, we repeat it, and as we repeat it, we find ourselves caught in a thicket of conflicted priorities. We in the United States speak of ourselves as peace-loving

---

* David Boulton, *Militant Seedbeds of Early Quakerism* (Landenberg, PA: Quaker Universalist Fellowship Publication, 2005). The two essays comprising this lecture can be read in their entirety at www.universalist friends.org/boulton.html.

people, even as we wage war. We define ourselves as a Christian nation, despite our collective appetite for war, which seems contrary to the life and ethos of Jesus. I bring this up not to denigrate our nation, but because these incongruities merit our serious attention. I also raise these issues to strip away the mystique of war and its tendency to cloud our reason and impair our long-term interests, and not just our interests, but the interests of the world and its future.

Though I wish it were otherwise, I have observed Quaker participation in war has increased especially among those American Friends whose theology has been influenced by Christian holiness, revivalism, and civil religion. This not only makes me wonder about the link between violence and religious zealotry but also about religion's power to corrupt our noblest intentions and make us forsake the values we first cherished.

When Does Violence Begin?

Let's return to the schoolyard fight I witnessed as a child. I left before the fight was stopped, but I later learned the two boys were taken to the principal's office and punished for their violence by being struck with a wooden board, the irony of which now astounds me. Though I wasn't present, I suspect our principal asked the boys, and perhaps other witnesses, who threw the first punch. This question is commonly asked when violence occurs, whether it is a schoolyard fight or a war between nations.

Our efforts to place blame invariably begin by discerning who threw the first punch. But does violence begin with the physical act, or does it begin when we first coerce another to act against his or her will?

Long before the first punch is thrown or the first gun is fired comes the effort to compel another to do our bidding. Thus, the commitment to nonviolence begins with a commitment to noncoercion. Think for a moment of the many ways coercion, or forcing compliance, is woven into the fabric of human affairs. Our government compels its citizens to pay taxes, not by appealing to our sense of charity and mutual responsibility, but by threatening fines and even imprisonment if we fail to cooperate. We often threaten our children with physical harm if certain standards aren't met. We are forced to participate in war, despite conscientious objections we might have. Or we are forced to pay for war through taxes, and face imprisonment or steep fines if we refuse. We often labor in unfair— sometimes inhumane—conditions, and when we organize, we are threatened with the loss of our jobs and the means to feed our children. We have created a world designed to punish or marginalize persons who question or reject our culture's assumptions and values.

Nevertheless, it is possible to rise above coercion and follow the dictates of conscience. I know a man, a fellow Quaker, who opposed paying taxes for war. Just as he couldn't take human life, neither could he pay others to do it on his behalf. He knew nearly half* his tax dollars were used for military expenditures, so he wrote the Internal Revenue Service telling them he would be withholding half of his tax dollars, directing that same amount of money to organizations working for peace. As you can imagine, this did not sit well with the IRS, and over the years he has been audited and money from his bank account seized, a process he welcomes since it gives him the opportunity to educate others about Christian pacifism. The worst things he imagined happening to him haven't come true. He hasn't gone to jail or lost his home. While his standard of living is not as high as that of his neighbors, he bears that cheerfully, pleased to sacrifice personal comfort for a greater global good.

Though his story is a dramatic one and his decisive action a step many of us, myself included, would fear to take, it speaks eloquently of the ultimate powerlessness of coercion. Once our deepest fears have been met and overcome, we enjoy a power and a freedom we have not known before. Too often we have been silenced or cowed by fears of retribution. But when we act, we discover our fears were overblown, and we are no longer held hostage by threats of retaliation. It is then we can begin living life powerfully and purposefully, living the prophetic lives God has called us to live.

If coercion is the root of violence, we must refrain from

---

* While thirty-seven cents of every tax dollar is directed toward military expenditures, additional monies are spent paying interest on past war debt, bringing the true figure of military expenditures to nearly 50 percent.

coercing or manipulating others to get our way, for that too is a form of violence meant to violate another's will or conscience. It is one thing to live one's life as a prophetic witness against evil. It is another matter entirely to take up a spirit of violence against that which we deplore. As for me, I am acutely sensitive when others coerce or pressure me, while I am less conscious of the ways I manipulate others to get my way. While I am not prone to physical violence, I have become adept at using subtler methods to accomplish my purposes. Because I have a facility for the spoken word, I sometimes have the ability to bring others around to my point of view. In the past, I understood this as a gift, but now I realize it too can be a form of coercion when used to manipulate others to achieve my goals. I have found myself shaping events at

> Defending righteousness makes us feel virtuous, even as we undertake that which is utterly lacking in virtue.

my Quaker meeting to get my way with little regard for the thoughts and feelings of others. My wife, were she not so kind, would tell you I have done the same thing in our marriage.

As a minister, it feels natural to speak about the will of God, but I have noticed a strong correlation between God's will and my own wishes. These might be the greatest temptations for those of us who are religious: the tendency to confuse our personal hopes for God's will and our propensity to lose moral perspective once we are persuaded of the righteousness of a certain act. More wars have probably begun in defense of righteousness than for any other cause. Unlike greed and the thirst for power, defending righteousness makes us feel virtuous, even as we undertake that which is utterly lacking in virtue. War is so horrible that we must first convince ourselves of the nobility of our actions. But having done that, we give ourselves permission first to coerce and then to kill another, and even feel honorable and godly while doing it.

Violence and Demonizing

I was seated in a restaurant sharing a meal with friends when a group of people seated at the table next to us began discussing President Barack Obama. They were talking so loudly it was impossible not to overhear them. Other patrons glanced at them, no doubt hoping they would get the subtle hint to moderate their volume. One of the women in the group said, "Someone just needs to shoot him."

A hush fell over the room. While I was still figuring out how best to respond, my wife turned to the lady and said, "That is unacceptable." A friend dining with us said to the woman, "There is no excuse for that kind of talk."

The woman rose to leave, saying, "Well, something should be done."

On later reflection, that woman's comment struck me as

selfishly wicked, in that she preferred the violent death of another over the perceived loss of privilege. I say "perceived" loss of
privilege because I doubt that her taxes were raised, that her guns
or property were seized, or that anything she had been warned
to expect had come true. Nevertheless, she believed herself to be
harmed by President Obama, despite all evidence to the contrary, and she wanted him gone. Hatred does not have to be

> We only have to *believe* someone poses
> a threat to us to justify their demise.

based on logic or actual circumstances. In fact, it usually isn't.
We only have to *believe* someone poses a threat to us to justify
his or her demise.

If coercion is the start of violence, shortly after comes the
effort to depersonalize and demonize those we fear and hate. It
would be unthinkable to most of us to kill fathers, mothers,
sons, and daughters. The woman in the restaurant would never
have blurted out, "Someone needs to kill Sasha and Malia's
daddy," for that would have conjured up an image of two little
girls bereft with grief over the loss of the father they loved, and
who but the sickest among us would wish to be the cause of such
pain? This is why we must first persuade ourselves that our enemies are less than human. Once that is done, we will support all
manner of evil against them.

The dehumanization of our enemies begins with our language about them. They are no longer human. During World War II, we derided the enemy as Japs and Krauts. When we went to war in Vietnam, we fought against slants and gooks. When we invaded Iraq and Afghanistan, we were fighting towelheads. Among violent Islamists, the people of the West are infidels. Just as soon as we create an "other," we create a hateful label and attach it to them, a label which invariably dehumanizes, stripping people of their dignity and making it easier for us to commit violence against them.

Some governments have recently acknowledged the role of language in human conflict and have moved to discourage hate speech. While such laws are often dismissed as political correctness, I believe they are an appropriate recognition of the destructive potential of certain words and are therefore a valid concern of those nations that seek a more just and peaceful world.

The Ritual of Scapegoating

When I was a child, a family with a daughter my age moved to our town. The girl was tall and awkward and had a poor complexion. By the end of her first day at school, she'd been given an unflattering nickname and targeted for ridicule and abuse. She lived in our town for three years and didn't enjoy a moment's peace at our school. I wish I had treated her with kindness, but wanting to impress others, I also taunted her. To this day, I can remember her nickname—but not her given name. I don't think I ever learned it. It was as if, once she was stripped of her name and assigned a derogatory label, it became acceptable to torment her. I don't recall any teacher coming to her assistance, nor anyone being punished for the abuse she received. It was as if the whole school had conspired to make her life a living hell, as if we needed someone to single out for scorn.

In the Hebrew Bible, in the sixteenth chapter of Leviticus, the ritual of scapegoating is described. The accumulated sins and offenses of the community were symbolically laid upon a sacrificial goat, which was then sent into the desert to perish. Today, we speak of scapegoats as those persons who are singled out and blamed for the misdeeds or failings of another. Though I wasn't familiar with that term when I was a child, it now seems an apt metaphor for our treatment of our classmate. Scapegoats are chosen because of their inability to punish or harm those who hurt them. They bear our anger and hostility because they are powerless to stand up to abuse, and that abuse always begins with a rejection of their humanity.

Our anger and hostility are often directed at those who stand at the bottom rung of our economy. When we first moved into our home, I hired a man to plant trees in our yard. He and his work crew, all Hispanics, arrived early one day, working through the morning to plant the trees. The crew worked diligently, seldom pausing to rest. Their work was exceptional, and they seemed to enjoy the work and take pride in their effort. I commented to the owner of the company that he was fortunate to have such good employees, and he agreed, noting they had worked for him for several years and had become his friends. When their work ended, I thanked each man and gave them each extra money for their work on our behalf.

Later that day, I went to the grocery store, where I was approached by a man who had driven past our home and seen the workers. He chastised me for hiring Hispanics when so many Americans were out of work.* I knew the man had been fired from several jobs because of his inappropriate conduct and that his own misfortunes had nothing to do with the willingness of Hispanics to do what many of us are unwilling to do. I also suspected the man wanted someone else to blame for the way his life had turned out.

This pattern of blame can reach epidemic proportions during times of economic difficulty. We become fearful and look around for someone to blame for our problems, an enemy responsible for our troubles. Unfortunately, when we die, the feelings of animosity do not die with us, for they have been passed on to our children, and in that way ill will accrues across the

---

* Several years ago I was speaking in Toronto, Canada, and used the word *America* when referring to the United States. I was quickly corrected by a woman in the audience who informed me that Canadians, as well as the other citizens of North, Central, and South America also considered themselves Americans. She was, of course, correct. It made me wonder whether not identifying our neighbors as fellow Americans makes it easier to view them as threats.

generations. This makes it probable, indeed inevitable, that animosity will go on and on, making reconciliation all the more difficult. Sometimes this leads to armed conflict, other times to deep and simmering hatred that identifies the despised as the reason for our decline. Once the man in my town identified Hispanics as the source of his problem, he refused to look more deeply at the real factors contributing to his economic struggle, including changing consumer demands, political opportunism, shifting economies and work patterns due to global trade, personal shortcomings, insufficient education or training, trade imbalances, mismanagement, corporate greed, and scarce resources, to name a few. Because a broader consideration of our situation requires effort and reflection, it is easier to single out a group or person responsible for our dilemma, allowing our anger to fester into hatred until violence seems a reasonable and justified reaction. It is all part of a pattern: the widespread human habit of blaming others for the difficulties and challenges in our lives. From there it is a short step to coercing others to do our will, then demonizing them, and from demonizing them, to harming them.

But What If...

But what if we understood others to be our companions and not our competitors? Wouldn't that be the beginning of peace? For once we comprehend that someone is our companion, we are less likely to coerce, demean, or diminish him or her. We realize that the *others* are committed to our well-being, and we are to theirs, and we come to depend upon them, as they depend upon us. Initially, we often don't realize this, causing us to fear and despise the very people essential to our well-being. We complain about Hispanics taking our jobs, but we would go hungry if they no longer picked and processed the fruits and vegetables we need to survive. The Chinese who came here in great waves to expand our rail system were disparaged by the very people who enjoyed the benefits of travel by rail. In China, the rural peasants who flocked to urban factories for jobs, who have made China's rapid economic expansion possible, are treated as the lowest of the low. The slaves who built our nation's capital and multiplied our nation's wealth were treated as mindless, lazy animals. Tell me, if they were so mindless and lazy, why did we covet their ingenuity and labor?

Those we depend upon the most are often met with contempt, until it occurs to us how difficult our lives would be without them. Then we realize they are our companions on the human journey, not rivals we must fear, and we begin to appreciate them in ways we hadn't before. We understand that our well-being is intrinsically connected to their well-being. We realize the struggles they face are similar to our own: our desire to support our families, our need for friendship, our hope the world will be gracious to our children. All the world over, the same dreams are dreamed. When we realize this, it becomes impossible to demonize another, for we are so connected to the other that to denigrate him or her is to diminish ourselves.

It is this shared humanity that underlies the Quaker testimony of peace. And not just our common humanity, but our

> When someone is our companion, we are less likely to coerce, demean, or diminish him or her.

shared divinity, the presence of God in which we all partake. We Quakers call this "that of God in every person." This shared Divine Presence brings us together, then binds us together, enabling us to care for one another. The alternative is tribalism and its jealous gods, whereby distinctions are forever drawn, suspicions raised, and boundaries guarded. This has been our past. It cannot be our future.

Why Is Peace so Difficult?

When I was a child it was my family's custom to watch the annual Miss America pageant on television. The program was so popular the other networks were loath to broadcast anything of merit at the same time as the pageant. So, like many Americans, we sat in our living room, viewing the proceedings to see how our state's queen would fare. The pageant became the source of a longstanding family joke, inspired by each contestant's customary response—"I would like to work for world peace!"—when asked what she wanted to do after college. The audience would applaud, the judges would nod their approval, and Bert Parks, the host, would beam at the contestant.

I envisioned Miss America visiting battlefields in her gown and tiara, standing between the warring factions, urging them to lay down their arms, which they, awed by her presence, would do. World peace sounded so attainable, so possible. Everyone I knew wanted it. We prayed for world peace each Sunday at church. Our political leaders proclaimed their fondness for it. Leaders of other nations pledged their commitment to world peace, saying if it were up to their country there would be no war. Musicians sang about it, poets wrote about it, students marched for it. Everyone wanted peace, or at least everyone I knew wanted it. Yet peace remained tantalizingly beyond our reach.

Despite this widespread longing for peace, many of the men in our town owed their living to conflict. They were kind men, most of them active in a church, volunteering in our community as coaches and civic leaders, and participating in various service clubs: the Optimists, Kiwanis, Lions, and Rotary. Yet every weekday they drove to the city to assemble the tools of war at factories in Indianapolis. Like most wage earners with steady employment, they were no doubt grateful for the opportunity to provide for their families. I wonder now how they felt about manufacturing goods whose purpose was to destroy human life in vast numbers, as efficiently and brutally as possible. Were they able to compartmentalize their lives to such a degree that they could pray for peace on Sunday, then design and build the tools of war on Monday? Did they ever pause in their work and wonder against whom the fruits of their labor would be used? Did they consider the sad harvest their labor would reap?

Do any of us consider our role in an economy structured for perpetual war?

Many gracious people purchase stock in companies that manufacture military goods. Pension funds, universities, municipalities, investment companies, banks, and even churches invest money in Lockheed Martin, Bechtel, General Electric, Honeywell, Raytheon, and Boeing, to mention a few. Because many of us place our retirement monies in mutual funds that own stock in these companies, we finance the production of weaponry, even if we are morally opposed to war. In fact, the companies that arm our nation and others are so large and diversified, it is impossible not to do business with them. The same General Electric that makes our toasters and clothes irons also manufactures the jet engines that power the F-16 fighter aircraft. Were you and I committed to not participating in a war economy, we could buy virtually nothing, so intertwined are the wares of violence with the production of everyday goods.

These same companies lobby our government to spend ever more tax dollars on the latest weaponry. They enjoy an access to our elected leaders the rest of us do not, influence their votes with money, and routinely circumvent the rule of law to prosper themselves. And prosper they do! The United States of America spends nearly seven hundred billion dollars, or $700,000,000,000, a year on its military. If we add the debt and interest owed on our past military expenditures, the yearly cost balloons to over a trillion dollars, or $1,000,000,000,000. This amount grows each year, and it does not include our nuclear weapons program, veteran pensions, or military assistance to other nations, which is considerable.

It matters little how many of us work for peace, desire peace, and insist on peace, as long as war and the preparation for it are so hugely profitable. In my own state of Indiana, in a wave of military base closings designed to reduce spending, 461 jobs were *added*.* Any effort to decrease defense spending is met with stiff resistance from legislators, lobbyists, and even foreign governments wishing to generate business for their own industries. The very term *defense spending* is a smokescreen, designed to obscure a practice that has little to do with our nation's defense and everything to do with an aggressive geopolitical posture and the hundreds of billions of dollars it takes to support such an empire.

How is this possible? How have we convinced ourselves this is an appropriate and reasonable expense given the challenges

---

* *2005 Defense Base Closure and Realignment Commission Report*

facing our nation and world? We have been led to believe it is money well spent, that massive and tangible threats jeopardize our well-being. To be sure, we live in an imperfect world, where troubled people can and do threaten our country. It seems prudent for nations to be able to defend themselves against violence and terror. But we have armed ourselves far beyond the actual threat posed by others, chiefly because we have been persuaded the danger we face is so significant we have no choice but to dedicate most of our resources to war and the preparation for it.

The corporations that reap billions of our dollars each year have a financial interest in stoking our fears, then devising expensive solutions to exaggerated threats. These solutions are always militaristic, since these companies profit little from the peaceful resolution of human problems. The peace dividend we anticipated at the close of the Cold War was modest and short-lived. It took no time at all to create a new enemy, to restructure our military to fight this enemy, and to once again place ourselves on a war footing.

To be sure, these companies employ a significant number of people, something they hasten to remind us whenever military cuts are suggested. Any effort to restructure our economy would need to create employment opportunities for the displaced workers. But there is no shortage of work needed in our nation—bridges are crumbling, factories sit empty, schools are decaying, inner cities and even suburbs are falling into ruin, mass transit is inadequate, public buildings are woefully outdated and lack current technology. In addition to these physical improvements, investment in human life is needed. Millions of mentally ill adults are homeless or inappropriately imprisoned, unable to safely and responsibly function without help. Single parents work long hours, yet they and their children live in substandard housing. Many senior citizens are warehoused in inadequate and impersonal accommodations, often victimized, seldom visited, given inferior medical care. The children of migrant workers are excluded from education, adolescents are forced into the sex trade, and many of our young people never realize their dreams or potential. And unlike every other advanced nation, millions of our citizens go without adequate health care.

When these human tragedies are brought to our attention, the answer is always the same: the problem is too great, and we lack the resources to help. This is, of course, a bald lie. Let us call it what it is. As a nation, we have decided to spend our considerable wealth on armaments and warfare at the expense of human dignity and well-being, education, and societal progress. Of course, we didn't all make that decision, but at significant points in our history that decision has been made, and remade, until it became our pattern.

Social scientists have noted how persons, when members of a group, will do things they would never do as individuals. Otherwise moral persons, when participating in a crowd, will forsake their morality to affirm the lesser ethic of a group or mob. Any group eventually succumbs to the lowest morality present within the group. This is another reason peace is so difficult to achieve. When we collect into groups or communities, our morality and ethical standards invariably decline.

The anthropologist Margaret Mead once famously said, "Never doubt that a small group of thoughtful, committed citizens can change the world. Indeed, it is the only thing that ever has." We have usually cited her words to inspire positive change, but the road runs both ways. It is also possible for a relatively

> To solve the problem of violence we must first solve the problems of gross profitability, unequal access to the ruling elite, and our tendency to let those who are ethically primitive determine our collective morality.

small group of people to change the world for the worse. A locksmith named Anton Drexler met a thirty-year-old struggling artist and intelligence agent named Adolf Hitler at a meeting in Munich in September of 1919. They would go on to tear the world asunder. Eighty-two years later, a handful of religious fanatics flew airplanes into buildings, killed nearly three thousand people, triggered two wars that caused hundreds of thousands of casualties, and sparked a global financial crisis. Peace is so difficult because it only takes a relative few people with a degraded morality, holding seized or granted power, to undermine our most noble wishes.*

To solve the problem of violence we must first solve the problems of gross profitability, unequal access to the ruling elite, and our tendency to let those who are ethically primitive determine our collective morality. Until those issues are resolved, violence will continue to haunt us. My belief in the gospel of human progress keeps me from despairing. Though the road to peace is difficult to traverse, it is not blocked altogether. God is on the side of peace, as are many good and thoughtful people all over the world. I believe the lion will lie down with the lamb and that swords will be beaten into plowshares. I might not be alive to see those things happen, but with all my heart I believe they will.

Inward and Outward Violence

Outward violence is not our only problem. It might not even be our primary problem. For what lies behind every act of outward violence is an inner sickness, a deficiency of spirit that has deadened the conscience. This moral malignancy permits one to profit with little regard for the well-being of others. Its goal is self-enrichment, self-satisfaction, self-aggrandizement, but always

---

* I find it somewhat ironic that in order to lead a small church, I was required by the seminary I attended to take psychological tests to determine my mental, emotional, and moral well-being, but someone can be elected to the American presidency without being required to undergo even a modest professional evaluation of his or her psychological health.

at the expense of another. Whether it seeks wealth, power, control, status, or some distorted sense of holiness, its hope is always the same: to gain by whatever means necessary its utmost desire, however squalid it might be. This inward distortion is the root of all violence, both emotional and physical. I know the brokenness well, because it is in me.

This brokenness is repeated the world over, whenever and wherever our highest ideals are forsaken. Such violence is done to the human spirit that our ability to live peacefully with others is compromised. Rather than working from a place of wellness and wholeness, we enter relationships and situations psychologically, spiritually, and emotionally damaged. Lacking inward peace, we cannot attain outward peace.

How is this inward peace found? I have a friend who believes a personal relationship with Jesus is essential for peace. He cites as proof the violence and upheaval in nations that aren't predominantly Christian. Though predominantly Christian nations aren't exempt from violence, he believes that is an aberration, not indicative of a general trend. I believe my friend, despite his many virtues, is unaware of the tendency of Christians to be just as violent as our fellow religionists.

I don't say this to denigrate Christianity or any other faith. Religion, when grounded in an ethos of grace, forgiveness, and reconciliation, can be a powerful tool in the struggle for peace. It matters little whether that religion is Judaism, Islam, Buddhism, or Hinduism. What matters is the believer's commitment to the highest ideals of his or her religion. But our tendency to believe our own religion or nation is uniquely qualified to attain a virtuous goal is part and parcel of our dilemma—we believe the best about ourselves and suspect the worst about others. This inward lack of trust breeds outward suspicion, generates ill will, and makes peace all the more unlikely.

Violence is a human problem with a human solution. I believe in a Divine Presence, but I see little evidence that God miraculously intervenes to bring peace. While some who work for peace are motivated by religious principles, even those who are

> Our tendency to believe our own religion or nation is uniquely qualified to attain a virtuous goal is part and parcel of our dilemma—we believe the best about ourselves and suspect the worst about others.

not religious have a role to play. The work of reconciliation begins when we believe in the inward capacity of people of all religions (and people of no religion), nations, and cultures to contribute to that end.

Inward wholeness is the foundation on which outward peace rests. We live from the inside out. Inward imperfections rise to the surface, just as magma pushes through to the earth's surface.

Consequently, the work of peace begins with a sincere consideration of our inner condition and its effect on our world. Does our greed create economic inequality? Do our prejudices make it easier to despise and exclude others? Do our religious beliefs breed distrust? Do we expect moral perfection from others with little awareness of our own ethical frailties? What inward deficiencies of our own push to the surface in our lives, causing harm to others?

There is a creek near my home that swells with water each spring, some years even sweeping away the large sycamores that line its banks. The source of the creek is a culvert in a farm field five miles to the north. I've stood alongside that seemingly insignificant culvert, amazed it can birth a torrent of water powerful enough to uproot a sycamore tree. But I know it is true. It is also true that every war ever fought, every tyrannical government ever to rule, every system of oppression ever devised, every clash between neighbors, every divorce, and every schism has had as its source the slightest trickle of a broken soul. If we wait until nations are armed and aggressive before acting, we have waited too long. If we wait until the gun is loaded, the warship sets sail, the warplane is fueled, and the army is massed at the border, we have acted too late. What must be healed is the hateful thought, the intolerant rhetoric, the laws that demean. The appeal of the Quaker virtues is found in their ability to stem the progression of violence. They change the mind, then the heart, and finally the world. They challenge the isms—racism, sexism, nationalism, sectarianism, fascism, and perhaps the most dangerous ism of all, fatalism, which tells us events are permanent and predetermined and we are powerless to change them.

Our Right to Be Rid of the Disease of War

Hateful words, prejudicial attitudes, and blatant ignorance create an atmosphere that makes violence not only possible but also inevitable. Outrageous statements intending to provoke and inflame are accepted as gospel truth, then repeated and embraced. When challenged, the speaker cites his or her right to speak. But what about the right of the rest of us to live in a society free of violence? What about our right to not reap the whirlwind of violence that ultimately follows hatred and ignorance? What about the right to not be lied to or about, and to not be treated unjustly? What about the right of our children and grandchildren to grow up in a world free of violence, where no government compels them to take up arms against their fellow beings? What about the right of nature to no longer absorb the horrific blows of bombs, to not have blood spilled on her ground, to not have her forests and fields shattered and broken by war? Why are those rights so seldom given voice in life's equation?

Think for a moment of the potential threats to our well-being and how our government has labored to resolve them. Several times a year, a tornado warning is issued for the area in which I live. I know of this hazard well before it exists because large amounts of money have been spent to detect, warn, and protect us from dangerous weather fronts. A network of meteorologists, scientists, government officials, and volunteer weather watchers cooperates to provide us ample warning. My house includes a basement, whose form and construction has been perfected over the years in order to provide maximum safety during potentially deadly storms. If our house collapsed upon us, firefighters, EMTs, and police officers would rescue my family and me in a timely manner, taking us to a community hospital built to provide health care for injured and diseased persons. This is neither remarkable nor rare. In every developed nation in our world, citizens have banded together to create similar systems.

But the government's effort to promote our well-being didn't end there. At one time, it was customary to spray farm fields with DDT to eradicate destructive insects. DDT was also used to successfully reduce the rates of malaria and typhus. But in 1972, fearing its long-term and harmful effects on the environment and human and animal life, the widespread use of DDT was banned in the United States. Many species of birds, including our nation's symbol, the bald eagle, have returned from the brink of extinction since DDT was prohibited. Similarly, other harmful chemicals have been outlawed or strictly regulated in order to protect human health. In our garages and kitchen cupboards are a variety of cleaners whose compounds have been tested to ensure their safety. Additionally, directions for their safe use, as well as recommendations for their proper disposal, have been prominently displayed.

We drive automobiles that have been engineered to protect not only our lives but also the lives of other drivers. If, after production, the car poses a threat to safety, it is recalled by the government, reengineered, and repaired. Some automobiles are designed to minimize harm to pedestrians in the event they are struck. I suspect that will soon become commonplace. Many states mandate the use of seatbelts, and most people would not dream of purchasing a car that failed to rank highly in safety tests. We pay a considerable sum of money for the many safety features on our automobiles, but believe it is money well spent and are grateful the government and automobile industry have worked together to dramatically reduce the number of traffic-related fatalities.

Each year, billions of dollars are spent developing cures for the maladies that threaten human health—cancer, neurological diseases, the physical decline associated with aging, and mental illnesses, to name a few. In the United States, more money per person is spent on health care than in any other nation. Approximately 17 percent of our nation's wealth is spent on health care.

These investments in our health and well-being demonstrate our collective decision to protect and preserve human life. Though our investments are imperfect and don't always accomplish their intended purposes, for the most part they reflect a shared concern for our mutual welfare.

In addition to these safety standards for our automobiles, household and agricultural products, and health-care practices, considerable effort has been made to regulate air and rail travel, construction, electrical generation, mine safety, road building and maintenance, and every other conceivable source of harm. But it is still legal to produce guns, missiles, and bombs whose purpose is the wholesale destruction of human life. Our government, the very entity whose purpose is to safeguard human life and liberty, continues to permit the manufacture of weapons whose sole function is to steal our life, liberty, and happiness. When will the day come that the manufacture of such robbers of life and joy is seen as a crime against humanity?

If violence and war were properly categorized as diseases, and it can surely be argued they represent as great a threat to

> If violence and war were properly categorized as diseases, we would devote vast resources to prevent their spread.

human life as any germ, we would devote vast resources to prevent their spread. But just the opposite happens. The companies producing weaponry are paid hundreds of billions of tax dollars each year. Can you imagine the outcry if botulism, E. coli, staph, or aspergillus were produced, distributed with only modest safeguards, and made widely available? Can you imagine any group demanding the right to own such pathogens as vociferously and mindlessly as the National Rifle Association argues for our right to own weapons designed to efficiently slaughter our fellow humans? Why does our society tolerate this risk to our well-being, while zealously safeguarding us from other threats? Three children in the United States died from lawn darts, which led to their ban in 1988. But 1,500 to 2,000 children under the age of seventeen are shot to death each year, and the manufacture of weaponry continues unabated. As of March 2013, the World Health Organization confirmed that there have been 622 human cases of H5N1 influenza, or bird flu, resulting in the deaths of 371 people since 2003. Panic ensued, and governments around the world invested billions of dollars to halt the spread of bird flu, while armament manufacturers report stunning profits. The perceived right to manufacture and own guns is so culturally ingrained we prefer the death of children over sensible restrictions on gun ownership, electing to office time and again the politicians who most fervently promise to protect the dubious constitutional right to bear arms.

Consider for a moment the makeup of the president's cabinet. In addition to the vice president, the following persons serve: the attorney general and the secretaries of agriculture, commerce, defense, education, energy, health and human services, homeland security, housing and urban development, interior, labor, State, transportation, treasury, and veterans affairs. Three of those positions—secretaries of defense, homeland security, and veterans affairs—concern themselves with wars and those who fight them. If we include the Department of Energy, which safeguards and maintains our nuclear weapons program, four cabinet positions focus directly on military programs.

Where is the advocate for peace and reconciliation in the president's cabinet? Who represents the interests of persons victimized by war? Who is present to urge our leaders to devote as much money and creativity to peace as we do to war? Who urges the leaders of warring nations to settle their differences justly and nonviolently, and makes such reconciliation possible? Who protests when American presidents declare war without the approval of Congress, and with it the implied consent of the People, who, though paying for war with our blood and loss, seem never to have a voice? Why, after 2,489,335 (and counting) American war casualties, is there not a Department of Peace?

Imagine if the interests of peace and reconciliation were equally represented at the highest levels of government. We could promote the study of war and its origins, seeking to understand it in order to provide alternatives to it. We could strengthen the role and reach of the United Nations, enabling it to live up to its charter of global peace and understanding. We could dramatically reduce the twin diseases of war and violence, or better yet, make them a distant memory, a part of our history but no longer a threat to our future.

A Plea for Peace

> "Peace I leave with you; my peace I give you. I do not
> give to you as the world gives. Do not let your hearts be
> troubled and do not be afraid." —Jesus of Nazareth

One recent summer day, I was sitting on my porch when two well-dressed young men approached my home asking if they could speak to me. Having seen them around town and recognizing them as two Mormon missionaries, I invited them to sit down on the porch and brought them iced water to drink, knowing they didn't drink caffeinated beverages.

Because I enjoy theological conversation and learning about other faiths, I asked them to tell me about their beliefs, which they did. Though I admired their commitment and appreciated their pleasant personalities, it was evident they were working from a script, and that neither one had the education or experience to talk at length about theological matters beyond their rehearsed lines. Our conversation ended with one of the young men warning me not to believe in evolution. Since we hadn't discussed that topic, I thought it odd, but I didn't comment. Instead, I thanked them for stopping by and told them they were always welcome in my home.

Curiously, since that day, I have been warned by other Christians to beware of evolution. While I know their objections, having heard them countless times, I don't understand them. I not only believe in the science of evolution, I am also counting on the principle of progress to usher humanity into an enlightened era. For a number of years, I believed God would finally and dramatically intervene on earth, initiating a world-wide reign of peace and justice. I no longer believe that. My Quaker morality will not permit me to assign to God the work of peace that rightly belongs to us. Will this reign of peace happen soon? Obviously not. Evolution, moral and otherwise, is a gradual, sometimes plodding, work, but it is an inevitable one. It is tempting to think peace will happen *for* us or *to* us, but it must happen *through* us and *because* of us. The peace Jesus leaves us is the capacity to forgive, the potential for reconciliation, and the example of determined grace. Jesus and other great spiritual teachers provide signposts pointing the way to peace, but they do not magically speak it into being.

Just as, in our evolutionary process, we've managed to over-come many obstacles that could harm us—disease, the effects of extreme weather, accidental injury—so must we take on the threat of war and violence. We must do this with the same re-solve and determination with which we have conquered other blights, recognizing violence for the global threat it poses. We must empower the wisest and most capable among us to wage war on war. Whenever rogue nations threaten the peace of their neighbors, we must not turn a blind eye toward their misdeeds; rather, we must go to them quickly and work for a resolution, so the cancer of war is checked. Whenever the leaders of a nation use violence against their own people or their neighbors, we must hold them criminally liable for their misdeeds, no matter their position or nationality. Violence is as contagious as any germ and to allow it to grow unchecked in one nation is to ensure its rapid spread to others.

Finally, we must surrender the notion of national autonomy and start to take seriously our global interconnection. Our world can no more afford 196 nations acting solely from self-interest, than the United States can afford its three hundred million citizens acting without regard for one another. Cooperation, mutual responsibility, and selflessness are as essential among nations as they are among families. The principle of autonomy, of nations acting as they wish with only their own interests in mind, must give way to a wider consciousness and a higher regard for collaboration and respect.

Consider the advances our world has made. We have discovered cures for diseases that once decimated our ranks. We cross the globe in mere hours; fly into deep space; harness water, wind, and sun to generate power; unlock the mystery of the human genome; build computers capable of processing billions of instructions in the blink of an eye; and create music and art that stir our souls. Yet we still resolve our human differences in the most brutal and backward fashion, like moral cavemen, as if no advances in human cooperation have ever been made. Why can't we commit ourselves to moral and ethical progress with the same enthusiasm and creativity that permitted our giant leap forward in science and technology?

Just as hatred and violence are learned, they can be un-learned. Nelson Mandela, the former president of South Africa, said, "No one is born hating another person because of the color of his skin, or his background, or his religion. People must learn to hate, and if they can learn to hate, they can be taught to love, for love comes more naturally to the human heart than its op-posite." We must nurture our innate capacity to love, affirm its value, and encourage its spread. This means rejecting politicians who champion violence so others will fear us, seeking instead leaders who make us so wise and gracious other nations want to emulate us. How much better our world would be if we no lon-ger fueled regional differences, pitting one nation against an-other in order to satisfy a short-term geopolitical goal that will later return to haunt us.

Our religious leaders must honor the best tenets of their faith, working for reconciliation, rather than behaving as if God is honored by the violence committed in his name. Just as some nations have taken a careful look at hate language, so must those who wield great power be held accountable for rhetoric that di-vides and diminishes the human family. Should one person's right to spew vicious hatred override the People's right to live in peace? How is any nation made better by the unchecked vitriol of a troubled and powerful few? Someday we will take seriously our forefathers' vision of life, liberty, and the pursuit of happi-ness, and when we do we will take seriously our right to live in peace and to have our resources directed toward goals which enhance and expand human life and dignity. This day cannot come too soon, for each passing year seems to draw us closer to irreversible conflict, when our capacity to love might well be outstripped by the twin desires of mindless vengeance and unbridled power.

Now, some forty years later, I walk past the playground and remember those two boys at war with each other and their troubled lives. I wish for them what I wish for all people: a life of peace and joy, unthreatened by hatred and discord. I believe such a life is possible, but it must happen through us and because of us, not to us and for us. We will have peace when we want it badly enough—and when we understand it is not an option but a necessity if humankind is to thrive.

Integrity

When I first began attending a Quaker meeting, my father, who had little interest in spiritual matters, said, "I like the Quakers. You can trust them. Lawson Barber is a Quaker, you know." Lawson Barber was a man in our town known for his integrity. This was as close as my father ever came to endorsing any religion, so his positive words about the Quakers meant a great deal to me, especially since he wasn't one and had no vested interest in their reputation. The Quakers I knew didn't boast about their virtues, at least not too much, so my awareness of their qualities unfolded gradually, as I got to know them. Of course, some Quakers seemed to value integrity more than others, but there nevertheless ran through the tradition a distinct regard for what Friends called truth-telling.

Some Friends I knew regarded truth so highly they frowned

upon my jokes, listening stone-faced, then saying, "That can't be true. Did that actually happen?" I would then be forced to admit a priest, rabbi, and St. Peter hadn't gone golfing, or a man and his talking dog hadn't walked into a bar. I quickly learned with whom I could joke and with whom I couldn't. Fortunately, most Friends I met were able to set aside their regard for truth long enough to enjoy a joke.

A fellow Friend and I were once talking about somber Friends who inspected every utterance under a microscope, and she laughed and said, "My dad was one of them. When I was a child, we were on vacation out west. We had stopped to get gas, and after he had paid the attendant, Dad said, 'See you later.' A couple of miles down the road, it occurred to Dad he probably wouldn't see the man later, so he turned the car around, drove back to the gas station and explained to the attendant he likely wouldn't see him again, so a good-bye would have to suffice."

"You're kidding," I said.

"Serious as a heart attack," she said. "And he didn't like jokes either. The upside was that he never broke a promise. Once he promised you something, he would move heaven and earth to make it happen."

Many of the Quakers I know have that quality in spades. Their word is their bond. One Friend I knew had pledged a significant sum of money to a charity, then experienced a serious financial setback. Rather than break his vow, he worked extra jobs for several years until his pledge was met. No one would have thought ill of him if he had gone to the charity, explained his situation, and asked to be relieved of his obligation, but that would have been unthinkable to him. I realize Quakers are not the only people with a high regard for truth, but I've met few groups who place it so squarely at the center of their lives. Early Quakers were known to greet one another with the question, "How does Truth prosper among you?" When early Friends wrote about truth, they capitalized the word, believing it merited their deference.

Despite my thirty-plus years of participation in the Quaker faith, integrity has not always come easily for me. Though I was taught as a child never to lie, I wasn't accustomed to the kind of introspection Friends encourage, the constant weighing of words to discern their accuracy. I found myself making promises I couldn't keep, exaggerating my accomplishments to gain favor, and sometimes even lying to protect myself against a perceived threat or challenge. I would tell myself they were white lies, minor untruths intending no harm. But in lying about small things, it became easier to lie about significant matters, so I had to develop the habit of being truthful in all things, no matter their scope. It is difficult to break established habits, and several times I've had to return to persons, confess an untruth, and ask their forgiveness. The embarrassment of that is a powerful corrective.

It is this growing awareness that Friends prize: the watchful attention to one's statements, the careful dissection of claims to discern fact from fiction—until truth comes naturally, as a matter of habit, with no inclination toward deceit of any kind. Such mindfulness isn't easy, but it brings clarity to one's life and is well worth the effort.

Why was truth-telling so important for early Friends? While our testimonies of peace, simplicity, and equality can be understood as prophetic responses to the misplaced priorities of seventeenth-century England, it can't be assumed that place and era were awash with liars, at least more so than any other culture has been. For the Friend, integrity was not so much a response to a perceived lack as it was the bedrock upon which all the other testimonies rested, for if one were judged to be dishonest, one's other virtues would be suspect. The testimonies of peace and equality were effective because the fidelity of their advocates was unimpeachable. A person corrupted by lies could not be trusted to conscientiously promote the high ideals of the Christian life. Quakers believed their credible witness to the gospel depended upon their reputation for integrity, that if they were dishonest in human affairs, they couldn't be trusted to speak truthfully about God.

This passion for truth-telling sometimes became the source of humorous stories about Friends. The story (ironically, I believe it is apocryphal) is told of a Quaker man and his friend driving through the countryside. A flock of sheep was grazing in a pasture, prompting the Quaker's traveling companion to comment, "It appears those sheep have recently been shorn."

The Quaker said, "Yes," then paused, thought for a moment, and added, "at least on this side."

While such precision might strike us as odd, haven't we all been disappointed and hurt by people whose word meant little, whose promises couldn't be trusted, who said one thing and did another? I purchased my first car from a man who assured me it was in excellent condition. Within a few weeks, the engine seized up, and I then discovered the previous owner had failed to properly maintain the car, despite his assurances to the contrary. I had borrowed money to buy the car, so I still owed money on it though it was no longer of use to me. When I told the man what had happened and asked for my money back, he refused to cooperate. I left his place of business angry and upset.

Shortly after that, I was given a traffic ticket. A friend told me if I contested the ticket, the matter would go to court, the police officer likely wouldn't show, and I'd win by default. I proceeded to do just that, writing the court to tell them I wished to challenge the citation. A court date was set. The police officer didn't show, but when the bailiff invited me to step before the judge and I pled innocent, I felt anything but innocent. I was certain that others knew I was guilty and that I was falsely claiming innocence in order not to pay a fine I honestly owed. The judge, because of the officer's absence, ruled in my favor, and the charge was dismissed. It was a hollow victory, and I left the courtroom ashamed of my dishonesty. By then, I would have gladly paid the fine to ease my conscience.

In that moment I realized I had acted no differently than the man who had sold me my car. Like him, I had lied for financial gain. Like him, I was reluctant to admit my guilt, either from embarrassment or greed. Like him, I was unwilling to right an obvious wrong. I also knew that since I had done precisely what he had done, I had forfeited my moral right to restitution.

Many years later I was present at a meeting in which two people were negotiating the sale of a home. The homeowner suggested a price for the home that I knew to be the appraised value. To my surprise, he then revealed the lowest price he would accept for his home, many thousands of dollars less than the stated price. I winced at his naiveté, certain he would be taken advantage of. The buyer said "I want to pay you what your home is worth" and offered him the asking price. In that moment I understood why the buyer was respected by all who knew him. I also understood that in matters of integrity it was better to go the extra mile than to fall short, for reputations, once tarnished, are difficult to restore.

As I reflect on that experience, I recall there was no hesitation on the part of the buyer. He didn't pause to weigh whether the savings in money would be worth violating his sense of integrity. Some are honest only when it doesn't cost, when they can burnish their reputation at little or no personal expense. They then make sure word of their virtue is widely known, citing it as evidence of their integrity. Many believe them and vote for them, follow them, buy from them, and otherwise elevate them, only to later learn their virtue could be turned on or off like a switch. But it is the instinct of integrity we seek, the honesty which comes automatically, which kindly and clearly speaks the truth no matter the consequences or cost. What we seek is for truth to come as naturally as breathing, without thought or pause, governed by the deepest, most basic, part of us.

Some fortunate people are born into a culture of integrity; they have known nothing but honesty and can't imagine choosing any other path. The temptations of deception never enter their minds. They were blessed with parents and friends who placed a high value on integrity and fostered it. Others have been born into families or cultures where deceit and trickery were encouraged, and perhaps even essential to one's survival. They learned at an early age to mislead and lie, believing truth would leave them vulnerable to threats and attacks. They understood dishonesty to be an asset, something that would better their lives. Steeped in that habit, it is difficult for them to alter deeply rooted behavior. This is why it is crucial to create cultures of integrity, so we learn the importance of truth from a young age.

When my older son was a child, he enjoyed answering the phone. On one occasion, a call was for me, but I didn't want to speak to the person, so I mouthed to my son, "Tell him I'm not home." This confused my son, since we had always taught him not to lie. He stood for a moment, pondering the situation, then said to the caller, "My dad told me to tell you he isn't home."

I spoke to the man, laughing off my son's remark as if it had been a joke, but after the phone call, I told my son he should have just told the man I wasn't home.

"You mean you want me to lie?" he asked.

"It's not really a lie," I said. "It's just something we tell people when we don't want to talk."

"Why can't I just tell them we don't want to talk?"

I asked my wife's help in explaining the particulars of phone calling to our son, but she refused. She said to our son, "You handled that very well. Your father could learn something from you."

We're never too old to learn about integrity.

Truth in Word and Deed

When the Religious Society of Friends was beginning, it was customary, as it still is, that when one testified in court he or she would have to swear to tell the truth. Quakers refused, not because they were unwilling to be truthful, but because they believed that swearing to tell the truth on one occasion suggested they were less than truthful on other occasions. English judges, in the mid-1600s, were not impressed with the Friends' reasoning, and many Friends were jailed for their noncompliance.

Jail was a familiar setting for many early Friends, due to their proclivity to share their honest thoughts about the king, the church, and God. When forced to swear allegiance to royalty, they refused. When ordered to pay tithes to a church they didn't belong to, they declined. When asked to recant, they repeated their theological assertions even more loudly, then put them in print in the event they hadn't been heard. They were prolific writers, publishing thousands of pamphlets in which they cheerfully pointed out the theological errors of others. They referred to themselves, rather immodestly, as Publishers of Truth. They weren't happy unless they were challenging, or otherwise irritating, a king or priest. They went to jail gladly, even exuberantly, believing it was an honor to suffer for the sake of truth. Eventually, the Friends would move to America and settle the colony of Pennsylvania, where they drafted a constitution to guarantee their freedoms to think, speak, write, and worship as they pleased. Nearly a century later, when Thomas Jefferson was casting about for a model for America's constitution, he would rely heavily upon Pennsylvania's *Charter of Liberties,* written in 1682 by the Quaker William Penn.

Just as Friends valued simplicity in dress, so too was their speech unadorned. They believed flowery speech intending to impress or curry favor was inherently dishonest, so they spoke to the king as they did the commoner. In an era stratified by class, this did little to win them influential friends. When William Penn addressed his father with the Quaker *thou* instead of the more deferential *you,* and refused to remove his hat in his father's presence, the elder Penn forbid his son entrance to the family home until his wife finally intervened.

Despite the difficulties blunt honesty sometimes created, it also proved to be a boon for Friends, many of whom, because of their reputation for integrity, became wildly successful business owners. Indeed, the Quaker penchant for integrity and fair dealing became so widely known and respected, other businesses employed the Quaker name despite having no connection to Friends. The most famous among them was Quaker Oats, and the most curious was a liquor named Old Quaker straight whiskey, whose bottle bears an ironic image of a teetotaling Quaker. The Quaker name and image have been used to sell, among other things: motor oil, flooring, cigars, animal lures, oatmeal, granola bars, cornmeal, canned fruit, windows, soap, spices, wax paper, coffee, flour, lace, hosiery, table syrup, evaporated milk, and a pilsner beer whose quirky motto was "The Beer That Makes Friends." Though it is good to have a reputation for honesty, it is a dubious honor to be immortalized by whiskey and granola bars.

Today, it is customary to enter a store and find prices clearly marked on each item. We have the Quakers to thank for that. Prior to their entry into business, the cost of merchandise was set at the whim of the seller. Often, the rich and powerful received a discount, while the poor were charged an exorbitant price for essential needs. Quakers established a fair price, charged everyone the same, and became known for the quality of their goods and work. They believed shoddy work was a sin and reflected poorly on their witness to God. Whether they were building houses or boats, making chocolate, administering financial institutions, practicing medicine or science, teaching, raising food, or weaving cloth, they did so with an eye for detail and quality, charging an equitable price, careful not to enrich themselves by exploiting others. Those Quakers whose professional or private conduct reflected poorly on their spiritual community were paid visits by their Quaker elders and invited to improve their reputations or leave. The typical Quaker meeting was no place for slackers or charlatans.

Several years ago, I was talking with a Quaker pastor whose meeting was preparing to build a new meetinghouse. The Friends met to discern whom they might hire to erect the building. One Friend suggested they should do their best to get the better side of the deal. After a pause, another Friend suggested they be careful to make sure the business venture was advantageous for all involved. She said, "Let us make this such a wonderful experience for the builder that afterward he would always be delighted to work with Friends." Many Quakers I know have a deep and abiding fear they might do something that would reflect poorly on the wider body.

When I first became a Friend, a man who attended our meeting had developed a reputation in the community for questionable business practices. It clearly distressed Friends that he was publicly identifying himself as a Quaker, and when he eventually left our meeting to become a Baptist, Friends seemed clearly relieved. At first, this struck me as religious snobbery, but now I think how seriously those people took their reputations for integrity and how painful it was when they saw their good name tarnished by one who claimed the same name. But more was at stake than their status. They also believed God's reputation was on the line, since inappropriate behavior by those claiming to be friends of God necessarily reflected poorly on God's character. (For that matter, I don't think the Baptists were all too happy with the man either.)

Seeking Truth

The Quaker affinity for truth went beyond word and deed; it was the basis of their spirituality. Unlike other Christians, the Quakers did not elevate the Bible as the final repository of truth. While they valued the Bible, incorporating its precepts into their daily lives, they were careful not to invest it with ultimate authority, believing no single book could capture the essence of God. They spoke instead of the Spirit from which the Scriptures arose and endeavored to seek and follow that same Spirit. Neither did they bend the knee to a church authority, hierarchy, or tradition in their search for truth. Indeed, they were suspicious, even dismissive, of religious authority, and felt quite free to say so, even visiting other churches to stand during worship and challenge priests. To put it mildly, they were not ecumenically minded, though later they would become more tactful in their theological exchanges.

They believed the search for truth was an appropriate goal of religion, and they felt quite free to look beyond the confines of Christianity. John Woolman, an American Friend, wrote in 1763 of his desire to visit Native Americans. "A concern arose to spend some time with the Indians, that I might feel and understand their life and the spirit they live in, if haply I might receive some instruction from them."*

They traveled widely, talking with any and all, sharing the Quaker understanding of truth with others, then listening carefully to their beliefs. One early Friend, Mary Fisher, traveled to Turkey in 1658 to speak to the Sultan Mehmed IV. He received her warmly, listened to her testimony, then shared his beliefs with her. She said of him, "He was very noble unto me and so were all about him…they do dread the name of God, many of them…. They are more near Truth than many nations; there is a love begot in me towards them which is endless…. Though they be called Turks, the seed of them is near unto God."†

Most Christians of that era happily denounced as pagans anyone outside the boundaries of the Christian faith. To be sure, the Quakers were not timid about sharing their beliefs, but they were also careful to listen to others. Truth, no matter its origin, was their goal. Woolman visited the native Indians, hoping to

---

* John Woolman, *The Journal of John Woolman* (Boston: Houghton, Osgood, 1879), 192.

† *Quaker Faith and Practice: Britain Yearly Meeting,* Reading 19.27 (London: The Yearly Meeting of the Religious Society of Friends (Quakers), 1995), http://qfp.quakerweb.org.uk. The term *Turks* not only applied to citizens of Turkey but to members of the Islamic faith.

"receive some instruction from them." Believing the pursuit of truth to be a worthy and lifelong endeavor, they cultivated the habit of listening not only to God in the silence of their worship but also to others.

It was a novel idea that the goal of a religion should be the fully engaged pursuit of truth and not the assent to specific doctrines or submission to an ecclesial authority. Religions, even today, usually ask us to believe something, then discern our spiritual well-being based on our unquestioned affirmation of creeds and doctrines. But Quakers believe God and truth are synonymous, that to find one is to discover the other. Consequently, their search for truth is not confined to theology. They embrace science with a passion, believing the secrets of the natural world, once revealed, will lead them to the Creator. They reject sacramental or ritualized religion, not because they believe that outward celebrations of an inward truth are inappropriate, but because they believe no fixed number of sacraments or rituals, be it two or five or seven, can adequately reveal God. In that sense, they are not anti-sacramental, but omni-sacramental; they believe all of life can and does point to God.

Because Quakers, like people of every religion, are sometimes uninformed about their founding principles, they sometimes grow upset when their theological conclusions aren't affirmed by other Friends. They have to be reminded that the search for spiritual truth is a journey whose end is always in front of us. The Buddhists have a belief akin to this when they say, "If you find the Buddha on the road, kill him." That is, if we have reached a settled understanding of divine truth, we can be assured we do not yet comprehend the God who is infinite in nature. Any god we claim to fully understand is not God, so we should put that god to rest and continue to seek. To seek truth is to commit oneself to the deepest reality, no matter where it leads, whether it affirms our religious beliefs or proves them wrong.

In the early 2000s, in an interview with a reporter, I questioned certain aspects of orthodox Christianity. Though I know many Christians have questions and doubts, I suspected that making my reservations public would cause me a measure of trouble, but as a matter of integrity, I believed it essential to be honest about my faith. The article was widely circulated and, as I imagined, I found myself at the center of a tempest, with a

> To seek truth is to commit oneself to the deepest reality, no matter where it leads, whether it affirms our religious beliefs or proves them wrong.

number of Friends in our yearly meeting demanding that my pastoral credentials, or recording, be rescinded. The matter dragged on for nearly a decade before the effort to rescind my recording wound to an end. I retained my recording for several reasons. People had grown weary of the controversy and wanted it stopped. Other factors were also at work. Even those who didn't share my theological views were concerned that any effort to censure or punish me would lead to a habit of theological censorship that would ultimately compromise our search for truth. One man, known for his commitment to orthodoxy, said to me, "I disagree with you, but if you are punished for seeking and speaking, the search for truth will be compromised."

This is often the ironic pattern in religious communities. Every effort to safeguard what is considered truth inevitably leads to the crippling of truth, for the very act of enshrining a belief and treating it as settled truth and infallible doctrine is to declare that the search for truth has concluded. Any religion with a regard for truth must resist every effort to bring its search for truth to an end. This includes the formation of creeds, which by their nature are presented as conclusive and indisputable. It includes authoritative statements made by church officials that are intended to stifle and silence discussion. It includes the elevation of any single book as the inviolate and inerrant Word of God, which is nothing but an effort to freeze the status quo and prevent the expansion of human equality, diversity, dignity, and growth. Any religion whose goal is truth must recognize the vast difference between *what we know so far* and *ultimate reality*, and try never to confuse the two. The first is a summation of what our best thinking has yielded to date, so is therefore never conclusive and is always being added to as our experiences and wisdom expand. The latter is that prize to which we aspire, that full awareness, that blessed perfection, which remains always and elusively in front of us, which we glimpse only in part. The apostle Paul alluded to this when he wrote of seeing in a mirror dimly.

As a Quaker, I believe the search for ultimate reality is not the purview of any one field. It is certainly not the sole province of theologians or the church, though they can contribute to the conversation. But theirs is only one voice among many. Philosophers,

> Any religion whose goal is truth must recognize the vast difference between what we know so far and ultimate reality, and try never to confuse the two.

scientists, ethicists, artists, poets, musicians, psychologists, astronomers, physicists, atheists, teachers, and others have a voice in the quest for truth and understanding. Any search for truth that concludes before all the evidence has been gathered is already corrupted. Our search for truth must be wide open, even when it takes us in directions we preferred not to go. This is the difference between propaganda and truth. Propaganda has a certain end in mind, and so it marshals and manipulates the "facts" to support its conclusion. Truth weighs evidence, seeks proof, is appropriately skeptical of authoritarian claims, welcomes questions, and doesn't fear dissent. Those committed to truth know it is sufficiently robust to defend itself. Propaganda resists close inspection and must be continually defended, lest it be proven wrong. Truth welcomes doubt and skepticism; indeed, it is best served by questions, suggestions, and corrections. Regrettably, most religions traffic in propaganda, not truth. This is not to say religious people aren't interested in knowing truth. Indeed, I've found just the opposite to be the case. When given permission to explore beyond the horizon of tradition, people of faith often engage the seeking process with energy and creativity.

It is our commitment to integrity and reality that enables us to welcome and appreciate people of other faiths and their perspectives. That is another difference between propaganda and truth. Propaganda seeks to convert the unbeliever, while truth seeks to hear them out.

Integrity Begins with Self-Awareness

The search for truth begins within the seeker, for if we are not honest with and about ourselves, we will find it impossible to be honest with and about others. In my midthirties, I became depressed and was urged by my wife to see a therapist. Though I had recommended counseling to others, I had never sought it for myself; I was embarrassed by my need and resistant to seeking help. Eventually, the pain of depression became greater than the pain of embarrassment, so I phoned a therapist, scheduled an appointment, and went, albeit reluctantly.

The therapist seemed uninterested in solving the problem of my depression, at least with the urgency I had hoped for. I wanted a quick fix, and suggested she give me a pill that would part my cloud of gloom. When she told me she wasn't qualified to prescribe medicine, I thought of excusing myself and leaving, but I feared it would be rude and decided to finish the session but not return.

When I got home, I told my wife I was healed, thanked her for her concern, and told her it wouldn't be necessary for me to return to the therapist. But by the next week, I was curious about what the therapist might have to say, so returned for a second visit. The second visit led to a third, when it dawned on me the therapist had hardly mentioned my depression. Instead, she had been leading me on a journey of self-awareness, and as she did, I began to feel my depression gradually lift. I began to see that I had gotten in the habit of blaming others for my feelings, wanting them to change to make me happy. Naturally, they were reluctant, and in some instances unwilling, to do that, and I responded by feeling angry, discouraged, and sad. The therapist helped me understand that I was responsible for my own feelings, responsible for my choices, and responsible for my reaction to others. When I finally got it, I felt tremendously alive and empowered; I stopped blaming others for my difficulties and began to take responsibility for my mood. Additionally, the therapist provided some practical guidelines on how I might do that. Though it was difficult to break what had been a long-held pattern, it was worth the effort, and eventually my disposition and outlook improved.

As I've reflected on this since, it occurs to me that every person I've ever met who is committed to integrity is simultaneously committed to knowing themselves, facing the truth about themselves, and accepting responsibility for their moods, actions, and reactions. The search for truth begins within the seeker. It begins when we endeavor to understand our motives and priorities, accepting nothing less than the truth about ourselves, especially when the light of introspection is painful and we don't like what we find. It requires little courage to believe the best about ourselves, but to acknowledge our need for growth is difficult. Facing ourselves squarely, scrutinizing ourselves instead of others, changing ourselves rather than insisting others change to suit us, is a solid first step in the life of integrity.

A woman in a church I once pastored had a difficult personality. She was what I call an injustice collector, one who is easily offended and prone to misinterpret statements. Though she was married, her husband busied himself with work and hobbies, mostly to minimize contact with her. Because she was active in the church, it was impossible for me to avoid being around her, though I found it frustrating. In meetings, she was abrupt, abusive, and difficult to trust. She quickly cycled through friends, wearing them out.

When challenged, she would explode, claiming the church didn't appreciate all the work she did on our behalf. She would threaten to leave, which many of us hoped she would do, though she never did. Finally, her boss, most likely exhausted by her abrasive personality, had her transferred out of state to another job. Six years passed. We heard nothing from her and didn't initiate contact ourselves. Then one Sunday she appeared at our meeting for worship. We scarcely recognized her. She was genuinely pleasant; she appeared calm and very much at peace. After worship, I sat down to visit with her, and she began by apologizing for the difficulty she had caused our congregation years before. She said her husband had left her, causing her to enter therapy where she had experienced significant and painful insights about herself, and as a consequence she had resolved to change and grow.

Intrigued, I asked her what the most important part of her transformation had been. She didn't hesitate. She said, "Learning to be truthful with every person, starting with myself." Then she paused, laughed, and said, "The second lesson I learned was that telling the truth doesn't mean I have to vocalize every thought that enters my mind."

"Truth is a wonderful virtue," I said, "as is tact."

By now you might be thinking I have strayed from my task of describing the Quaker way, but let me explain how self-awareness and truth-telling intersect in a tradition we Friends call the queries.

The queries are a series of self-directed questions we employ to evaluate our emotional, spiritual, and relational health. Some of the queries are centuries old, others of them newer, speaking to more modern concerns and insights. They vary from one yearly meeting to another, though there is often overlap. Some Friends write personal queries to aid in their own development. Many Friends use them as a guide in worship and daily reflection. Ideally, they are read one at a time, in an unhurried manner, allowing the question posed to be absorbed and considered. I have known some Friends to keep a single query at the center of their attention for an entire year, allowing it to gradually modify their behavior in a desired direction.

The following queries, gleaned from the previously cited *Quaker Faith and Practice: Britain Yearly Meeting,* offer us insight into the nature of queries. They include:

- Are you open to the healing power of God's love?
- Do you try to set aside times of quiet for openness to the Holy Spirit?
- Do you follow Jesus's example of love in action?
- Are you open to new light, from whatever source it may come?
- What unpalatable truths might you be evading?
- Do you respect that of God in everyone though it may be expressed in unfamiliar ways or be difficult to discern?

- Do you cherish your friendships, so that they grow in depth and understanding and mutual respect?
- Do you recognize the needs and gifts of each member of your family and household, not forgetting your own?
- Do you faithfully maintain our testimony that war and the preparation for war are inconsistent with the spirit of Christ?
- Are you honest and truthful in all you say and do?
- If pressure is brought upon you to lower your standard of integrity, are you prepared to resist it?
- Do you keep yourself informed about the effects your style of living is having on the global economy and environment?

Given the Quaker fondness for writing and introspection, it's no surprise that hundreds of Quaker queries have been written. Some, penned for a special moment or event, lasted only a season. Others, speaking to a universal yearning, have endured for centuries and continue to be used and appreciated today. They range in subject from stewardship, spiritual health, earth care, race relations, justice, prayer, marriage, sexual orientation, raising of children, treatment of the elderly, our relationships with governments, peace, simplicity, and our standard of living, to name a few.

The point of the queries is simple: to encourage honest self-evaluation in light of our Quaker values and priorities. They focus scrutiny on ourselves and away from others. We do not use the queries to assess anyone's life but our own, casting light on those areas of our lives we need to develop. Consequently, the queries are employed in our journey toward wholeness, which is the next dimension of integrity I invite us to consider. At the end of this book, you'll find a thirty-day spiritual exercise that employs Quaker queries. I hope you find them helpful in your spiritual journey.

Integrity and Wholeness

When I was in elementary school, I learned about fractions and whole numbers and was introduced to the word *integer,* which is a Latin word meaning *whole* or *entire.* If you look at the word closely, you'll notice its resemblance to the word *integrity,* which derives from the same Latin word. We also speak of *integration,* by which we mean, among other things, combining several parts into a unified whole.

To say a person has integrity means several things. Most commonly, we mean the person is honest, that his or her word can be trusted. Thus far, that is the working definition of integrity we've been using, and most likely the definition that comes first to mind when we hear the word *integrity.* But there is another level of meaning that has to do with the *integration* of our values and lifestyle. In that sense, to say we have integrity is to say the separate parts of our lives combine to form a unified whole. What we believe is consistent with how we live. Our beliefs influence the work we choose, the way we use our time and spend our money, the relationships we form and the goals to which we aspire. This integration is critical for inward peace. Without it, we experience a split-mindedness, a separation between who we wish to be and who we are. This divorce between our ideals and actions make wholeness and happiness difficult, if not impossible.

I know a young man who was a gifted student; he won a scholarship to an engineering school, where he graduated with honors. He then was offered a job at a company that produced targeting systems for the military. Eager for employment, he accepted the offer, moved across the country, and began working. Initially, he was pleased with his job, which paid well and was located on the East Coast, a part of the country he'd always found interesting. Then our country went to war, and while watching the news one night, he heard the system he'd worked on mentioned by the reporter. In that moment, his work went from being a philosophical abstraction to a specific contributor to human suffering. He returned to work, but he did so with a heavy heart, unable to square his vocation with his values. Eventually he was no longer able to bear the discrepancy between his peaceful nature and the violence inherent in his vocation. He resigned his job and took another, making less money but experiencing greater satisfaction.

He likened his work in a job inconsistent with his values

with trying to fit together two pieces of wood not intended to be joined. "I just kept hammering away at it," he told me, "thinking if I tried hard enough, everything would eventually fall into place. But it never did."

I have found myself in similar situations, trying to unify disparate segments of my life into a coherent whole. Invariably, I discover that when my life is out of balance, it means I have made a decision inconsistent with my values. Not long after my first book was published, I was offered a significant sum of money to speak at a dinner sponsored by a political organization. Anxious about money, I agreed to speak, even though I was morally opposed to the social goals of the group that had invited me. As the date neared, I became tense and unsettled, angry at situations and persons unrelated to the event. I actually hoped I would become so sick I wouldn't be able to speak, then I could return the money and be done with the matter, my conscience intact. Unfortunately, I woke up the morning of the talk feeling especially healthy. I gave a humorous, but innocuous, speech, even though I believed they needed to be challenged for stances they had taken that I believed were injurious to others. After the speech, I gave the money away, vowing never to profit from organizations whose goals I found morally objectionable. For some time afterward, I felt ethically superior, then realized I had failed in almost every regard. Though I disagreed with the group's views, at least they had made no secret of their beliefs. Nor had they kept their views to themselves in order to make money, as I had done. Even though I had given the money away, it felt to me as if I had accepted thirty pieces of silver to forsake my dearest values.

What stands out in my memory is the brokenness I felt during that time. When we understand integrity as the unification of the different aspects of our lives, then we will experience the absence of integrity as brokenness. It wasn't until I began to reflect on money and its role and power in my life that I was able to acquire some sense of peace and resolution. Because of that event, I discerned that money is the most beguiling temptation for me: I am far more likely to risk my integrity for money than for any other reason. Other people might be similarly tempted by power, fame, sex, or prestige. When we understand what seduces us, we can be especially cautious when tempted to risk our integrity for some fleeting pleasure. This doesn't mean I respond appropriately whenever I am tempted by money. I have not yet reached that level of maturity. I may never. But I am more deliberate than I used to be when money is involved. I am more likely to seek counsel, or to remind myself that my needs are being met and that turning down money will not jeopardize my family's well-being. We preserve our integrity and wholeness when we are aware of what threatens it and then choose to act deliberately and prudently when tempted. When we fail to do this, we disintegrate, creating a chasm between who we are and who we wish to be.

The Fallacy of Situational Integrity

Several years ago, an acquaintance of mine was in need of a new vehicle, so put his used car up for sale. While negotiating with potential buyers, he "forgot" many of the car's deficiencies, suggesting it was in much better shape than it was. In fact, he had recently taken the car to his mechanic, had been told it needed expensive repairs, and then decided to sell it before it cost him additional money. He justified his duplicity by pointing out that everyone involved in the sale or purchase of a car knew the customary rules of honesty didn't apply. The car was purchased by a low-income family after my acquaintance had assured them it was in fine condition. Within a short time, the car broke down, the family could not afford repairs, and they were in worse shape than before, having spent all their money on a car that no longer ran. I would have been really disappointed with my acquaintance if I hadn't once done the same thing.

Many times we rope off areas of our lives, telling ourselves that integrity in a particular facet of our lives isn't essential. People who claim to value honesty aren't forthcoming on their tax returns, fail to mention the true condition of something when selling it, assure a police officer they weren't speeding, falsify expense reports, remain silent when a cashier mistakenly charges them a lesser amount, or lie about their child's age to gain a discount. We justify our dishonesty by pointing out that the wronged party will never miss the money—that they are too big and successful an entity to even notice.

Our farmhouse was once broken into and robbed. When I phoned our insurance to report the theft, he told me to buy replacement items and send him the receipts; I would then be sent a check for reimbursement. When I mentioned the break-in to a friend, he jokingly said, "Now you can get those new woodworking tools you've always wanted."

I laughed, but after we parted company I thought about how easy it would be to replace the things stolen with items of higher value. I knew my insurance agent trusted me and wouldn't question my purchases. I thought of the billions of dollars my insurance company made each year and told myself they would neither notice nor miss the extra money I would spend. I thought of how much money I spent each year in insurance and how few times I had filed a claim. Because I am especially prone to worry

> Integrity does not present one face in public and another in private.

about money, I was greatly tempted to fudge the figures. In the end, I submitted an honest appraisal of my loss, but I was sorely tempted to do otherwise.

Integrity isn't conditional, nor does it take into account the wealth, reputation, or relationship of the wronged party. People who would never lie to a family member sometimes feel quite free to mislead a stranger, a business, an organization, or the government. But integrity, because it arises from one's inner morality and spirit, isn't situational, requiring honesty in one situation and forsaking it in another. There is a seamless nature to integrity that transcends situations and relationships. Integrity does not present one face in public and another in private. It delights in transparency, having nothing to hide. I hope the day might sometime come when that will come naturally and easily to me.

The Decline of Institutional Integrity

The seamless nature of integrity means we are called to act with honesty in both our personal and public roles. By public roles, I mean our participation in society's structures, such as governments, economies, political systems, educational organizations, and religious communities. It is no secret that the bedrock institutions that form our society no longer enjoy the trust and esteem they once did. We have borne witness to the corrupting effect of money in our political process, have seen the fall of prominent preachers and priests, have watched our educational systems fail us, and have seen financial institutions we once thought impregnable collapse under the weight of greed and fraud. I cannot think of even one societal pillar untouched by scandal. Even the once-venerated family doctor is seen by many to be grasping, caring more about wealth than health. In my own work as a pastor, I have become acutely aware of the suspicion that now falls on clergy following revelations of sexual abuse in the Roman Catholic community. Of course, these abuses transcend the Catholic community, though it has suffered more negative publicity than others. When the Quaker meeting that I pastor built a new meetinghouse, I instructed the builder to install a glass window in my office door, knowing the days of closed-door trust were over.

This mistrust, whether warranted or not, has a corrosive effect on our communal efforts, causing us to distrust our fellow beings before we have even had the opportunity to know one another. We adopt a posture of wariness, questioning the integrity of others whether or not they have given us sufficient reason to doubt their motives or character. This mutual suspicion diminishes trust, making healthy community nearly impossible.

Near my home, a gas station began requiring payment before the pump would operate. It troubled me that someone with whom I did business would assume a lack of integrity on the part of their customers, and I began purchasing my fuel elsewhere. I am increasingly reluctant to engage in exchanges that begin with mistrust, since I believe that distrust and suspicion grow exponentially when unchecked by reason, faith, and optimism. Though not always successful, I try to undertake each interaction with a spirit of trust until that trust is violated. Very few times in my life has my trust in another person been misplaced. What I have discovered, time and again, is that when people are trusted, they become trustworthy. They are determined to merit the faith others have placed in them.

One time I hired a man to work on our home. Shortly thereafter an acquaintance of mine warned me about the man's shoddy work and his lack of integrity. I had already paid the man a portion of his wages, materials had been purchased, and I realized it would be difficult to hire anyone else to do the job. When the man arrived for his first day of work, I welcomed him into our home, stated my confidence in his ability, and gave him a key to our home to allow him easy access to the areas needing work. He responded beautifully, doing excellent work and even lowering his price when the materials cost less than he had estimated.

This experience caused me to wonder if the perceived decline in institutional integrity could be—at least in part—a consequence of our suspicion and cynicism. When we expect politicians to care only about money and power, money and power become their priorities. Time and again, I have seen people rise, or fall, to the level expected of them. When I was in college, I enrolled in a class in statistics. In high school, I had done poorly in math and logic and so warned the professor I likely wouldn't do well in the class. "You will make an A in my class," she said. "And by the time we're done, you will love statistics."

"I hope you're right," I said, though I was very doubtful.

Her prophecy proved accurate. I made an A and thoroughly enjoyed the class. I am certain if my professor had said, "This is a difficult class. You will probably not pass it," I would have failed. But because she expressed confidence, I was determined to confirm her faith in me. The same holds true for most all humans. Trust is repaid with trust, integrity repaid with integrity, kindness with kindness. The tragic loss of confidence in our society's bedrock institutions is not the sole fault of those in positions of leadership and power. It is also the fault of those who have expected so little from politicians, clergy, educators, businesspersons, government officials, and police officers. We have expected so little, so have been offered little in return.

Another danger of lowered expectations in matters of institutional integrity is our inability to compromise. When we participate in society's institutions, we assume the people on the other side of an issue—whether the other side is a political party, pro-life or pro-choice, believers in another denomination or religion, workers in a different agency or department, or members of the US Chamber of Commerce or the Sierra Club—are inherently untrustworthy. We attach a moral value to every issue, implying those who disagree with us are not only wrong but also immoral. Because we think they lack integrity, we are reluctant to compromise with them, seeing it as acquiescence to evil, and our society becomes deadlocked, unable to solve the problems facing our world. So it is that our deepening suspicion of institutional integrity—together with our unwillingness to work within and through institutions to accomplish some greater good—is crippling our capacity for healthy growth and transformation.

It wasn't always so. At one time, in the not too distant past, persons could and did disagree, sometimes strongly, without questioning the other's integrity or sincerity. People were simply seen as different, not dishonest.

Though I cannot cite a specific event that brought this camaraderie and goodwill to a close, I can say matters and mind-sets have changed. The trust and goodwill that once lubricated our social discourse seems absent. If I believed this were a permanent fixture, an irredeemable feature unlikely to change, I would be discouraged. Instead, I observe the sweep of history and note how pendulums swing from one side to another. I believe when citizens and leaders understand the high cost of polemic mind-sets, they will endeavor to end them. I believe institutions, and the people who constitute them, can learn and grow and be worthy of our trust. I believe this because the alternative is too dreadful to imagine—a broken, corrupt world, devoid of goodness, unable to transform or inspire. To give up on our collective efforts to better the world is to give up on goodness and beauty and love. There are those who have done that, but I cannot. Neither, I believe, can God.

Integrity and Community

One of the most powerful and potent substances known to humankind is the Clostridium botulinum toxin, often found in raw meat. One teaspoon is enough to kill millions of people. Fortunately, death is altogether avoidable if meat is heated to 185 degrees Fahrenheit for at least five minutes. I often think of this when grilling hamburgers. I also think, when considering that wily toxin, how similar it is to the dangerous potency of dishonesty and how even a small amount can prove fatal to human relationships.

When I was a teenager I worked at a grocery store several nights a week and every Saturday. One Saturday—a beautiful spring day, to be fair—I didn't want to work, so I phoned in sick, telling the owner I had the flu. The next day I went to Quaker meeting where I saw the owner of the grocery store, who commented on my robust appearance. It was quite obvious I had lied, and it was also obvious that I had lost the trust of the owner. Afraid I might be fired for lying, I heaped on more lies, telling him how sick I had been, and marveling at the apparent miracle of my quick recovery. He didn't fire me, but I also knew he no longer trusted me. I suspect he was waiting to see how I might resolve the issue. Several months passed; I felt ashamed every time I saw him, and I finally went to him and apologized. He forgave me immediately, but I suspect he still harbored some doubts about my integrity.

I still remember, all these years later, the fear that caused me to pile one untruth on top of another. Fear is a common obstacle to integrity. We sometimes lie or withhold information when we anticipate the truth will anger others. One lie leads to another until a wall of deceit has been erected, protecting us from a perceived harm. The harm does not have to be real. It only has to exist as a possibility in our minds for us to instinctively act to protect ourselves, even to the point of lying. So spouses will lie to one another, children to their parents, students to their teachers, citizens to police officers, taxpayers to the IRS,

> Truth and integrity are not an option; rather, they are an obligation for those seeking the higher life.

and even, in matters too painful to face, we lie to ourselves. Truth is integral to healthy community, but deceit borne of fear erodes the possibility for life-giving relationships.

Every religion with which I am familiar places a high priority on truth and integrity. For we know without these virtues our growth, liberation, and maturity are impossible. Truth and integrity are not an option; rather, they are an obligation for those seeking the higher life. "We shall know the truth," a great rabbi once said, "and the truth shall set us free."

Community

Our first community is never one we choose. It is chosen for us, usually by our parents and the accidents of biology. It consists of our parents, siblings, grandparents, aunts, uncles, and cousins. Though we had no choice in the formation of this community, it is often the most enduring and enriching community many of us ever experience. While some families are unhealthy and must be avoided in order to preserve our well-being, far more families become the central communities around which we happily orient our lives. It is surprising how often the one community we had no choice in joining becomes the most significant community many of us will ever know.

Our First Community

I once heard it said that all the communities we later form are attempts to recapture the family community we wish we could have had, or once had and wish to enjoy again. Given that, it is no surprise that members of certain church communities often refer to one another by family titles. When I was young, I addressed the priest at our Catholic church "Father," while the abbess in the local convent was known as "Mother Superior." My next-door neighbors attended a Pentecostal church where they were known as Brother and Sister Smith.

It is impossible to overemphasize the importance of our family, our first community. Even if our early experiences with family were negative and abusive, we remain connected to them, if only because the effects of their conduct remain a part of us, continuing to exert an influence upon us. As the moon causes the ocean's waves to rise and ebb, so does our family of origin exert a pull upon our lives. This never changes, even when we attempt to divorce ourselves from our family of origin. While it is possible to be less negatively affected by a corrosive family life, the experience can't be dismissed or forgotten. The destructive consequences of a dysfunctional family can't be undone, but they can be overcome by a constructive, life-giving community, which is why the church or any spiritual community should make the formation of healthy relationships a top priority.

Friends and Community

The practice of community was essential to early Friends, and it remains so to this day. Even our name indicates the centrality of community in our faith. We are the Religious *Society* of Friends. While our religious society encourages individual growth, it does so as a collective activity, seeking and promoting the betterment of individuals within the context of a gathered people. While our society's goal is the betterment of the self, it is not a narcissistic self toward which we aspire, but a connected self, rooted in a loving, transformative community. It is because of our participation in the *we* that we learn to be an *I*.

In our communities, we not only learn how to love and grow, we learn how to forgive, negotiate, compromise, yield, or stand our ground. Imperfect communities teach us how to love

> It is because of our participation in the *we* that we learn to be an *I*.

and care for others, how to listen, and how to share our deepest thoughts and feelings. They teach us consideration for others, the limitations of the self, and again, even most importantly, how to be an *I* in the midst of a *we*, how to maintain healthy individuality when the pressure to conform to a majority is strong. Those persons most able to stand apart from their community, even as they remain within it, are the people most likely to initiate positive change within a community. I think of people like the Quaker John Woolman who labored, at times reviled and alone, to end slavery, first in the Society of Friends and then in our nation. Our country reveres the memory of Martin Luther King Jr., who even as he planted himself squarely in the American community, was able to stand beyond it and prophetically articulate a nobler way. We can only change the communities we are a part of, though the dictates of our conscience might require us to speak prophetic truth to our community.

When I first joined a Quaker community, a fellow Friend felt led to demonstrate against President Carter's decision to reinstate selective service registration. This followed on the heels of the Soviet Union's invasion of Afghanistan and was intended to send a stern message of disapproval to the Soviet Union. My fellow Friend believed military intimidation carried in it the seeds of war, resolved to work against it, and notified our Quaker community of his decision. Some in our community, suspicious of the Soviet Union, suggested the man remain silent. Others urged him on, citing Quakerism's historic witness to peace. It soon became clear we would not reach consensus. Then an elderly woman spoke, saying, "If our Friend's intention is God's will, if God wills peace, then we should all join in it. If this young man's resistance is wrong, if God does not will peace, then we need not feel led to affirm what this young man is doing." After a period of discernment, it was agreed that God willed peace, not violence. The meeting then encouraged our fellow Friend not only to proceed with his leading but also to include others in our religious society in his effort. "We are not lone rangers," the elderly Friend reminded us. "What we do, we do together."

This regard for collective work dates from our earliest days. In our first decades, Friends voluntarily underwent arrest in order to provide solace and support to imprisoned Friends. In the American South, entire Quaker communities numbering hundreds of people migrated north en masse to begin new towns and meetings in regions untainted by the slave trade. One such meeting was the Trent River Monthly Meeting in Jones County, North Carolina, who left behind their homes and businesses and moved together. The meeting I belong to, Fairfield Friends Meeting near Indianapolis, was part of the 1820s mass exodus of Friends. One of our ancestors was in his eighties at the time of the exodus, and when asked what he hoped to contribute to a new Quaker community, he purportedly answered, "I'll start a new cemetery." He lived a short time after the journey and is believed to be the first Friend buried in our cemetery.

The Quaker theology of worship hinged upon community. Friends understood worship to be a collective effort, requiring the presence and participation of others. An especially powerful worship was referred to as a "gathered" meeting, when everyone's sense of divine leading dovetailed.

In this religious society, no one person was to be elevated above others. All stood before God equally and together. All discerned God's truth and will together. All labored for peace and justice together. Significant progress was made on many fronts due to the Quakers' ability to marshal like-minded people to work together for a great cause. When a Friend would venture forth alone to speak and travel among other Quaker communities, he or she was given a traveling-minute, a written endorsement from their local meeting introducing them to other Friends, a Quaker seal of approval, if you will. No Friend traveling to speak or visit among other Friends would have done so without the support of his or her spiritual community. This sense of community served as a corrective against those who would act unilaterally or impulsively. It was not always a fertile ground for prophetic voices, since would-be prophets first had to win over their fellow Friends, but once agreement was reached, they would undertake great challenges—the eradication of slavery, prison reform, women's rights, political freedom, feeding the hungry, peace-making, and economic justice.

Occasionally our fondness for community led to a distorted sense of unity. At one time Friends who married outside the Quaker community were "read out of meeting," a quaint term for expulsion. Deviations in dress and conduct were frowned upon and often cause for discipline or eldering, including the loss of one's right to speak in meeting for worship. I can imagine few things so forbidding as finding a handful of somber Friends on your doorstep, intent on setting you straight. The 1600s was not an era known for religious tolerance. The civil authorities showed no hesitation in punishing perceived heretics. One Friend, James Nayler, had a hole burned through his tongue with a hot iron and the letter *B* (for blasphemer) branded upon his forehead. Nayler's fellow Friends had little sympathy for him, because of Nayler's unfortunate decision to enter the city of Bristol on a donkey while his admirers carpeted his path with their clothing. Though he denied any messianic aspirations, as his punishment he was lashed through the streets of Bristol until his skin hung in tatters, then imprisoned for many months.

Released from prison, Nayler journeyed north to be reunited with his wife and children, but while on the way, he was the victim of a brutal attack by robbers. Carried to the nearby home of a Quaker physician, realizing his end was near, Nayler uttered perhaps the most eloquent deathbed testimony ever given:

> There is a spirit which I feel that delights to do no evil, nor to revenge any wrong, but delights to endure all things in hope to enjoy its own in the end. Its hope is to outlive all wrath and contention, and to weary out all exaltation and cruelty, or whatever is of a nature contrary to itself. It sees to the end of all temptations. As it bears no evil in itself, so it conceives none in thought to any other. If it be betrayed, it bears it, for its ground and spring is the mercies and forgiveness of God. Its crown

is meekness, its life is everlasting love unfeigned; it takes its kingdom with entreaty and not with contention, and keeps it by lowliness of mind. In God alone it can rejoice, though none else regard it, or can own its life. It is conceived in sorrow, and brought forth without any to pity it; nor doth it murmur at grief and oppression. It never rejoiceth but through sufferings; for with the world's joy it is murdered. I found it alone, being forsaken. I have fellowship therein with them who lived in dens and desolate places of the earth, who through death obtained this resurrection and eternal holy life.*

That such an impressive statement could be made from one's deathbed suggests either that Nayler was an incredibly resilient orator or that an eyewitness with a knack for embellishment was present. Whatever the case, the forty-four-year-old Nayler died estranged from many in the very community for which he had labored so faithfully. Today, he is remembered less for his occasional excesses and more for his eloquent testimony of the Christian faith.

The life of James Nayler illustrates the best and worst of Quaker community. Before his spiritual misjudgments, Nayler enjoyed the deep respect of his fellow Friends. In his Quaker

---

* *Quaker Faith and Practice: Britain Yearly Meeting,* Reading 19.12 (London: The Yearly Meeting of the Religious Society of Friends (Quakers), 1995), http://qfp.quakerweb.org.uk/qfp19-12.html.

community, he found support, a sense of belonging, and encouragement. After the passion of his faith became an embarrassment to Friends, he discovered firsthand the expectations of unquestioned conformity, the tendency to punish and isolate those who act unilaterally, and the stifling of individual creativity and insight. Even the founder of Quakerism, George Fox, nursed a long grudge toward Nayler and resisted efforts toward reconciliation. In reading accounts of their meetings, one senses a vein of envy in Fox's treatment of the charismatic Nayler. Alas, this too is often a downside of community: the twin passions of jealousy and resentment. No human community is purely good or purely evil. They exist on spectrums, their virtues and vices contending for primacy. It is our duty to heed the better angels of our nature, as Abraham Lincoln would say, and lean always toward virtue, lest our vices lay waste to our highest ideals.

The Role of Community in Discernment

I spoke above of the Quaker ability to marshal like-minded people to work together for a great cause. Nowhere is this more evident than in the process of discernment, when Friends gather to make and implement decisions affecting the community. Accustomed to the top-down pattern of religious authority, I was surprised as a new attendee to be invited to attend a church business meeting where I was asked my thoughts on a matter the meeting was facing. Though I can no longer remember the topic, I do recall feeling deeply listened to, as if my insight mattered to the meeting. A woman seated at a table (I would later learn she was called the clerk of the meeting) had opened our meeting with a prayer, explained the business at hand, then listened carefully as people spoke, taking care to allow ample time for quiet reflection and discernment. This, I would learn, was Quaker consensus.

In this process, the sum of the group's vast experience and the full range of insight are put into play. When one person lacks specific knowledge, another in the group often fills the void. Of course, in any group are persons who overestimate their wisdom, consider themselves experts on a broad range of matters, and dominate conversations. A skilled clerk can deftly corral their participation while working to elicit the perspectives of more introverted persons. The best clerks can make all feel heard and valued, while weaving the disparate elements into a unified and motivated whole. Each person will leave feeling his or her contributions were valued, while also appreciating the thoughts and gifts of others.

Consensus helps avoid the hard feelings that often accompany voting. The goal is not for any one side to win, but for all to seek God's will together. This process cannot be hurried. I have sometimes found myself frustrated in a meeting for business, wishing decisions could be quickly made. I remind myself that careful deliberation up-front saves time and trouble in the end. Additionally, when the winner/loser outcome inherent in voting is avoided, it is more likely all will work together to implement the agreed-upon plan. Because everyone has a stake in the matter, everyone labors to accomplish the goal.

In consensus, we learn how to deliberate, compromise, and consider the full breadth of an issue, thereby avoiding the limitations of all-or-nothing thinking. We see matters not only through our own eyes but also through the eyes of others. We are slower to speak and more apt to listen and solicit the views of others. The spirit is one of cooperation, not contention.

In my years as a Quaker, I have seen intractable problems whose solutions, in my mind, seemed hopeless. When held to the light of community discernment, the layers of difficulty were peeled away and the core issue recognized and addressed. I hold great stock in individual creativity and the inventiveness often exhibited by the lone person toiling in solitude on the next grand breakthrough. But I have also seen the wisdom of many eyes and minds brought to bear on a problem, and I know that carries with it an unmatched energy and inventiveness when skillfully marshaled by a perceptive clerk.

Consensus decision making has the power to make us careful listeners, thoughtful speakers, deliberate thinkers, and creative problem solvers, the very traits that serve us well in marriage, work, relationships, and life in general. Consensus decision making cultivates transferrable skills that serve us well in every facet of life. What good is a religious faith that teaches us only how to behave in church? Ideally, the practice of our faith should influence and strengthen every facet of our lives. When community and the lessons we learn in it are a priority, all of life is transformed.

Making Community a Priority

When I was a child, I once went on vacation with my family. We were driving through a small town in Wisconsin when my father stopped to fill our car with gas. Inside the gas station was a soda pop machine, filled with bottles resting in near-freezing water. Our car lacked air-conditioning, it was August hot, and we begged our parents to buy us each a bottle of pop.

"If you hurry and pick one, you can each have a bottle," my father said. This was back in the days before a few companies had monopolized the soft drink industry, so the machine was filled with a variety of drinks—orange, grape, root beer, cherry, cream soda, lemon-lime, and the requisite cola. Our options were so plentiful that choosing just one was akin to torture, but we eventually made our decisions, prodded along by our father, then climbed in the car to resume our journey.

I drained my drink, then thoughtlessly tossed the empty bottle out the window into the roadside ditch. My mother scolded me. "What if everyone threw their trash out the window? What kind of world would we have?"

This was my mother's mantra, ever present through my childhood: "What if everyone did that?" I spent most of my early years having to imagine all the world littering, interrupting, wasting food, stealing, complaining, fighting, and saying "ain't." To be human was to bear always in mind one's connectedness and responsibility to others.

When I moved from home in my late teens, I hoped to never hear that phrase again. Then I took up company with Friends, the people who likely invented it. My mother was raised Catholic, but she spoke the language of Quakerism. It is the language of imagination, of reflection, of always wondering what the world would be like if everyone did what you were doing, be it good or ill. To be a Quaker is to always understand yourself and your actions in terms of the world. It is an invitation to reflect, not simply react, to keep before you the question, *What would the world be like if everyone did what I am doing?*

I didn't come to the Quaker way easily, and I was especially resistant to the testimony of pacifism. I remember once talking about it with a man in our meeting who had spent World War II in jail. While he had agreed to serve the country in a nonviolent capacity, his draft board had been adamant that he carry a gun. When he refused, they pressed charges; he was found guilty of violating the law and was sent to prison. I had little sympathy for his position and asked, "What would happen if everyone had refused to fight? What would we have then?"

"I suppose we would have peace," he said. He went on to say there was no other way to achieve the world we wanted than to live right now in the world we wanted. For many people that seems idealistic, perhaps dangerously so, but for the Quaker it is a matter of integrity to live out the ideals of faith, even when others aren't. Indeed, the Quaker would argue that when others are not living up to the ideals of peace, simplicity, justice, and integrity, it is even more imperative for Quakers to model the possibility of such a life.

I was taught that when community was forgotten, one became predisposed toward evil. Community was the safeguard against destructive behavior and the corrective against selfishness. One did not participate in war, not only because Jesus had told us to love our enemies but also because war threatened global harmony. One lived simply, not only because it focused the mind but also because simplicity helped ensure there would be enough for everyone. One spoke the truth, not just because lying was a sin but also because mutual trust was essential for healthy community. One was open to new ideas and alternative points of view, not only as a guard against arrogance but also because tolerance and mutual respect were vital to human relationships.

To be a Quaker is to always see oneself in relation with the world, answerable not only to God but also to humanity and to history. In my early years in the Society of Friends, I was asked by a man in the meeting to visit a local jail with him, not to preach to the inmates but to befriend them. It was not presented to me as an option but a requirement. Though I was hesitant to go, I could see no way out, so found myself visiting the jail once a week. It was interesting that even the people who had been removed from society were, in that Quaker's mind, still a part of our community and not to be overlooked.

Quakers worry inordinately about how history will judge us and what future generations might think of us. We live in fear an injustice will pass unnoticed, so we appoint committees to

> To be a Quaker is to always see oneself in relation with the world, answerable not only to God but also to humanity and to history.

read and study, then prevail upon legislators, presidents, and dictators to act justly. Because we believe all are part of the human community, we have no qualms about speaking with anyone if we think good might result.

In 1938, the Quaker Rufus Jones traveled to Germany to meet with Reinhard Heydrich, one of the chief architects of the Holocaust. Though Jones was not granted an audience with Heydrich, he and two other Friends met with Heydrich's representatives, whose hearts were softened because of the Quakers' work feeding millions of refugees in Germany and the rest of Europe following World War I. Jones, with the passion and nerve the morally upright often possess, asked permission for them to travel among the Jewish citizens of Germany to learn their condition, and was granted permission and access, permitting them to ease the suffering of some Jewish citizens and facilitate their immigration to other nations.

Not to boast, but I have seldom engaged with a group of people so thoroughly involved in the world. We're poking our noses into every corner of it, suggesting improvements, like hovering mothers bent on civilizing their errant children. The Quaker William Penn observed that "true religion does not draw men out of the world but enables them to live better in it and excites their endeavors to mend it." When I joined the Religious Society of Friends, I was visited by three elders who came to gather my statistical information—date and place of birth, my parents' names, and other riveting information someone might one day find useful to know. (Quakers love few things more than collecting and discussing biographical data.) After we had dispensed with the information gathering, one of the elders asked, "What will be your ministry?"

"Excuse me?"

"What ministry is God calling you to?" she asked.

"I don't know that God is," I said.

"God calls everyone to some kind of ministry," she said. "Perhaps we can help you discern what God wants you to do."

This was my first inkling that Quakers weren't going to let me coast; they had no intention of letting me occupy a pew without some effort on my part to save the world. They were true to their word. I've been with Friends ever since, and they've never hesitated to tell me what God wants me to do. Service and community are essential to the Quaker way.

There Is No Isolated Sainthood

When I moved from home to live by myself, my interest in spirituality dramatically increased. Time and energy I had once devoted to relationships were now dedicated to my spiritual development, which I welcomed. Immersed in Bible study and prayer, I found myself growing not only more confident of my religious knowledge but also proud of what I perceived to be my spiritual maturity. I began to think God was pleased with me to a degree God wasn't pleased with others. I didn't tell others this—it was a secret between God and me—but I nevertheless was convinced of my holiness. When my pastor mentioned the difficulty of the Christian life, I arrogantly believed anyone who found the Christian way difficult shouldn't pastor a church.

Three years passed, and with each passing year my pleasure and pride in myself grew. Then, on a summer day in my twenty-first year, I met my future wife. We began dating, and two years later we married. Though my wife was, and is, a kind and gracious person, I began finding my saintliness tested. I discovered I could be edgy, short-tempered, and impatient. Not always, of course, but often enough to make me question my piety. Though I continued to study the Christian faith, my expanded knowledge didn't translate into faithfulness. In fact, after my wife and

I had children and they began to talk and express their own opinions, I seemed to become even more estranged from my Christian ideals. I was no longer the saint I had imagined myself to be.

Discouraged, I shared my concern with a trusted friend who listened, then said, "Anyone can be a saint who lives alone. The real test of sainthood is living wisely and graciously with others."

Behind every saint is a community. Think for a moment of our spiritual heroes—Mother Teresa, Thomas Merton, Martin Luther King Jr., the Dalai Lama, Mohandas Gandhi, and others. What do they have in common? Each of them was immersed in a spiritual community that honed their faith, clarified their thought, tested their resolve, and provided support.

Mother Teresa received much public acclaim, but behind her stood the Missionaries of Charity. Thomas Merton wrote beautifully of the spiritual life, but he did so alongside the Trappists at the Abbey of Gethsemani. Martin Luther King Jr. enjoyed the support of his peers in the civil rights movement, the Dalai Lama is surrounded spiritually and physically by his fellow Buddhists, and Gandhi had the faithful support of the Sabarmati Ashram. I think of my own life and the spiritual communities that have enriched my faith and expanded my mind. I can't begin to imagine how different my life might have been without the people I've loved, who have loved me in return.

This isn't to say my relationships have always been free of difficulty and strain. Sometimes they have been very demanding, even painful, and I have been tempted to leave them. But I have cultivated the habit, after my initial discouragement and anger wear off, of asking myself, *What can I learn in this circumstance? What does this situation have to teach me that I haven't yet grasped?* In chapter 27 of the book of Proverbs, it is written, "As iron sharpens iron, so one person sharpens another." Community provides us the opportunity to be sharpened, which is to say it makes us more useful for a given purpose. Most often we are sharpened by struggle and strain, not ease and comfort.

A friend of mine enjoys the hobby of blacksmithing. Occasionally, I will visit his forge and watch him fashion something from iron. He does this using intense heat, anvils, hammers, vises, and brute strength, producing an object of great beauty or usefulness. I am not advocating the use of force and violence, but we do ourselves a grave disservice when we flee from the hard knocks of community life. There is, of course, a vast difference between letting ourselves be used as punching bags by unhealthy persons and communities, and fleeing whenever we are faced with the challenges common to every life. Unhealthy communities not only bludgeon us; they also make us feel as if the deficiency is ours, as they refuse to accept responsibility for their sickness. Healthy communities remind us that life can be difficult and support us properly and lovingly, but they don't hurry to fix our problems while they still have something to teach us. They permit us to be properly sharpened by the pressures of life.

I have had the privilege of meeting and knowing many

wonderful saints in the course of my life. Each one of them could point to a community and say, "They made me what I am." As iron sharpens iron, so one person sharpens another.

The Slow Dying of Community and Its Remedy

When I was growing up, it was customary for the citizens of our town to gather in the courthouse the night of elections and watch the election results being posted on a blackboard as the votes were phoned in from polling places around our county. The courthouse was packed well past midnight, until all the votes were counted. Campaign losers would congratulate winners with a smile and a handshake. Winners would take pains to appear modest, crediting others for their victory and saying kind things about their political rivals. It was almost always the case that the winners and losers knew one another well; in fact, in many instances they were friends, and sometimes even related.

In the summer months, in the evening hours, we would gather at the town park to watch the Little League games. The bleachers would fill, lawn chairs would line the fence, and people would occupy the shade underneath the trees. Across the street from the baseball diamond, teenagers would swim at the town pool or shoot baskets at the basketball court. After the baseball games concluded, we would end our day at the Dairy Queen, then play under the street lights or sit on our porches and visit with our neighbors.

In July, the county fair would be open, its barns and midways surging with townspeople and farm families for ten days. Stores would close early each day so their owners could enjoy the fair. Churches would suspend evening activities while the young and the elderly and those in between inspected the livestock, rode the Ferris wheel, and examined the produce, baked goods, and handicrafts.

I realize, even as I recall these sepia moments of my childhood, not everyone enjoyed such an upbringing and that in many ways my growing-up years were an anomaly. But I would hasten to add that the rich community I enjoyed was replicated on city stoops, in neighborhood pubs, in local churches, and in food markets. Today, these venues that once populated our small-town and city life seem increasingly rare. Air-conditioning has brought us indoors, away from our breezy porches. Facebook, video games, and reality TV have taken the place of neighboring. Organized youth sports and travel teams have replaced sandlot ball games. Political differences have become so rancorous that a gentle conversation about social issues is next to impossible. Because we are absent from one another, we are forgetting how to be in community, how to talk with each other, and how to care for our neighbors. Consequently, we are failing at one of Christ's greatest commandments: to love our neighbors as we love ourselves.

In the midst of this decline in community stands the church. But the church is not the unifying force it once was.

The culture wars have divided us. In my own town, the conservative and progressive pastors no longer join together in a ministerial association, something they once did with mutual joy and benefit. Theological differences are no longer viewed as opportunities to learn, but as positions to attack and defend. The middle ground, once vast, well populated, and accommodating, is fast disappearing.

Any effort to heal our land, whether sacred or spiritual, must first address our frayed sense of community. Unfortunately, there is profit to be made in division. Power is conferred upon those who stoke the fires of separation; rivers of money are diverted their way, as are influence, devotion, and fame. If at one time there were a stigma attached to belligerence, that time has passed. The consequences of our division are obvious. We are no longer willing to work together to solve the problems facing our communities, nation, and world. The compromise necessary for such work is now seen as a weakness, as a concession to the enemy, even when that enemy is our neighbor. Worse yet, there is now a spiritual quality attached to our views, so that those who differ from us are seen as heretical and displeasing to God. Those Christians who support a woman's right to choose are denounced by other Christians as unfaithful and sinful. Those Christians who cannot in good conscience remain silent about abortion are dismissed by other Christians as hateful and ignorant. Were we to lift out the word *abortion* from the previous sentence, we could just as accurately and easily replace it with the words *the right to bear arms, welfare, gay rights, tax increases,* or the like.

Sadly, we Quakers have not distinguished ourselves in this regard. Many of our meetings now identify themselves as progressive or conservative, as post-Christian or Christ-centered, as Spirit-focused or Bible-based. No matter our place on the spectrum, we claim to hold the authentic Quaker position, citing past Friends to defend our theological positions. The same is

> I can think of no nobler and more vital work for the church to undertake than the building of healthy communities in which differences are appreciated and not feared, where past truths are honored and emerging wisdom encouraged.

true for almost every denomination. It remains to be seen whether this chasm can be bridged and the church can be a healing agent in our fragmented society. But I can think of no nobler and more vital work for the church to undertake than the building of healthy communities in which differences are appreciated and not feared, where past truths are honored and emerging wisdom encouraged.

Historically, there have been two churches. One church has

used its power to suppress positive change. It has valued its own power over justice, freedom, and peace. It has enshrined the status quo with lofty proclamations, denouncing as heretical any challenge to its authority. This is the church that pits nation against nation, oppresses entire peoples, relegates women to a subordinate role, and works to deny homosexuals equal rights before the law. Though it claims the title of church, indeed often refers to itself as the true church, it has corrupted the gospel and damaged the human community, all in the name of God. Regrettably, this church transcends denominations. Its adherents can be found in every Christian tradition. It is, in nearly every moral sense, the caboose on the train of history—the last to adopt positive change, especially when that change threatens its power.

But there is another church. It too has existed throughout history. It is found wherever and whenever peace, joy, and compassion carry the day. Undergirding it, in the words of Nayler, is "a spirit...that delights to do no evil." It labors not for its own glory, but for the well-being of all people everywhere. It rejoices when the marginalized are included, when the slave is freed, when the despised are embraced. It sees in its fellow beings not sin and separation from God but potential, promise, and connection. Wherever people love, it is there. Whenever people include, it is present. Whenever people join together in a spirit of compassion and inclusion, this church feels at home, for those virtues have been its priorities from its earliest days. This church has existed since the time of Jesus, but its benevolent spirit predates the Nazarene. It is not the province of any one denomination; its adherents can be found in every movement and every faith. While others bluster and rant, its members go quietly and cheerfully about their ministries, determined to bring heaven to earth. This church seeks to learn, understand, and include. It is of the world, loves the world, and welcomes all people as its brothers and sisters. Where borders separate, this community straddles the partition, refusing to let arbitrary lines rule their conscience and conduct. They are, in every sense of the word, members one of another. Community and compassion are their bywords.

I learned this way among the Quakers, even as they sometimes neglected its standards. I remain a Friend because their dream of this high community continues to enchant and embrace me. I will die surrounded and cared for by this community, connected always by the bonds of mutual love.

I write about the Quaker way because I believe in its power to create such a church and such a world. I believe the testimonies of simplicity, peace, integrity, community, and equality, when properly lived out, have the potential to create heaven on earth. This requires more than our lip service or intellectual assent. It requires the commitments of our hearts, souls, strengths, and minds to this high way. I believe this compassionate, inclusive church can be a microcosm of this transformed world and the means by which such a world is achieved.

Equality

I grew up six blocks from a Quaker meetinghouse, pedaled my bicycle past it every day delivering newspapers, but I had little curiosity about what happened inside its doors. It wasn't until the seventh grade, in Mr. Ellis's history class, that I learned anything about Quakerism, when Mr. Ellis taught us about the 1681 land grant of Pennsylvania by King Charles II of England to the Quaker William Penn, and the Quaker involvement in the abolition of slavery, including our participation in the Underground Railroad, which relocated thousands of fleeing slaves from the slave states of the South to the northern states and Canada. Though the first event provided Quakers a foothold in the American colonies and ensured our rapid migration from England to America, I didn't find it interesting and soon forgot it. Our defiance of the law and the inherent excitement of helping slaves escape to freedom captured my imagination, and the lesson stuck. I think that might be true for many Friends, who cherish our historic efforts for equality and justice.

This uniformity in status and treatment was, and is, a hallmark of the Quaker witness. How did equality become an important element of Quaker practice? What was the underlying principle driving our passion for justice and equality? From our earliest days, Friends believed deeply in the universal presence of God in all people. To denigrate or diminish people because of their gender, nationality, race, or religion was not only a denial of justice but also a denial of the presence of God within them. Consequently, women played a formative role in Quakerism, speaking and traveling in ministry, serving in leadership, working to alleviate the suffering of the poor and imprisoned. Many of the pioneers of public education and women's suffrage were Quakers, striving to ensure everyone enjoyed equal access to these rights, which they believed to be God's will.

In the stratified society of 1600s England, the rich and powerful were accorded honors and privileges seldom extended to the working class. The refusal of the Quakers to tip their hats to their social "betters," their rejection of language that conferred status, and their challenge of customs intended to keep the poor and powerless in their place were a deep source of irritation and offense to those in power. While many Friends were imprisoned for blasphemy and other dubious infractions, it seems more likely the case they suffered imprisonment for annoying powerful people. As glad as the Quakers were to come to America, the English aristocracy were probably just as pleased to be rid of them.

I know Quakers who love nothing more than hearing of some injustice or inequality, large or small, they can protest. Sometimes we even picket one another. A dear Friend, in the last year of his life, protested against the rise of ecclesial hierarchy at our worldwide gathering, bearing a sign that called Quaker leaders to task for their perceived movement toward authoritarianism. Within a short time, he had persuaded other Quakers to march with him, picketing the very gathering they had traveled thousands of miles to attend.

I know other Quakers who live together as husband and wife but refuse to marry until gays and lesbians are accorded the right to marry. When the world eventually comes around to their way of thinking, they will go in search of other inequities to challenge. One Friend, after his state of residence granted homosexuals the right to marry, took up the issue of health care, protesting the disparity of medical care between the rich and poor. Someday that matter will be resolved, and he will go in search of a new injustice. These are not isolated events among a handful of Friends. There are people like this in nearly every Friends meeting I've ever known, driven by a keen sense of justice and equality.

Inequality as a Social Disease

I mentioned earlier that when I was a teenager, I worked at a grocery store. One evening, while I was sacking groceries, a cashier made a derogatory remark about black people. The summer before, I had met an African American teen at a youth camp; we had shared a dormitory room for two months, worked side by side, and become close friends. When I heard the cashier comment unfavorably about black people, I was upset by her bigotry and challenged her. She dismissed my concerns with a wave of her hand and continued to use inappropriate language when talking about African Americans. Several months later, I had the opportunity to meet members of her extended family and understood a bit better the roots of her intolerance. She had been steeped in intolerance from her youngest days.

I remember asking my mother how seemingly nice people—the young lady was perfectly pleasant in every other regard—could be racist. "Some people," my mother said, "can't feel good about themselves unless they feel superior to someone else."

About that same time, I began reading the Bible and noticed the same pattern of intolerance repeating itself. Brother was pitted against brother, tribe against tribe, religion against religion, nation against nation, the prophets of Yahweh against the prophets of Baal. Intermarriage between tribes was forbidden, and in some instances it was punishable by banishment and even death.

On one occasion, during a discussion at church, someone noted the pattern of discrimination in the Hebrew Scriptures and said, "Thank God it isn't like that anymore." But in every direction I turned, I saw that discrimination was still with us. I saw how the blacks lived in one part of the city and whites in another. I noticed how the poor were left out of important decisions affecting their lives, and that while they could vote, they were seldom invited to serve in positions of leadership, nor were their opinions actively sought. Indeed, for the most part they seemed invisible to the rest of us. They didn't belong to our civic organizations, weren't invited to our parties, didn't enjoy the same access to health care, and, lacking social contacts, weren't considered for the same jobs. When something was stolen, the poor were presumed to be the culprits. If there had been blacks in our town, I suppose they would have suffered the same fate. After Martin Luther King Jr. was assassinated, I remember certain adults joking about it. In short, I saw little evidence the prejudices and animosity described in the Bible had come to an end.

The situation has improved since my childhood, but in my travels I still see relatively few blended neighborhoods. I see Hispanics working jobs no one else wants, poor children in inferior schools, the wealthy benefiting from governmental largess while deriding the recipients of welfare, the poor dying in disproportionate numbers in any war, the infrastructure of the inner city decaying while beautiful parks are being built in the suburban communities that ring our cities. When I visit prisons, I meet ethnic minorities and the poor, and I am reminded once again of the harsh treatment meted out to those lacking the resources and contacts to obtain justice and avoid imprisonment. I know a man who defrauded a business for nearly a half-million dollars. His father was actively involved in politics, and he hired a well-connected attorney close to the judge who tried the case. Though the man was found guilty, no serious effort was made to recover the stolen funds, nor did he serve any time in jail. If the man had been poor, black, or Hispanic, and had robbed a thousand dollars from a liquor store, I have no doubt he would still be in prison.

In addition to these inequities, there are systemic biases that keep some up and others down. Our federally mandated minimum wage is so far from a living wage that tens of millions of industrious people, working full-time, remain in humiliating poverty. While there is a minimum wage, there remains no maximum wage, so corporate executives receive outrageous salaries, far above their actual contributions to society, while their employees work extra jobs to make ends meet. The children of those executives attend the finest schools, enjoy the best health care, and spend their lives in the rarified air of privilege and wealth, cultivating relationships and associations that ensure a continued cycle of power, prestige, and wealth.

Our system of taxation, written by the wealthy, permits the rich to reduce their debt to the very society that has made their success possible. We now have a parasitic class within our country—and it is not the poor who stand on street corners, unable to find work, receiving a meager sum from the government to stave off starvation. It is the rich who grasp and grab their share—and not just their share but also the portions of others, as if money flowed in an infinite river. They remind me of the rancher who lived upstream, diverting the water to his fields, leaving those downstream to starve and die of thirst.

Then, with stunning audacity, the privileged speak in hallowed tones of the American Dream, as if their hard work alone made their success possible. In fact, many were born on third base, yet they believe they hit a triple, and think they merit the cheers of the crowd. When these inequities are challenged, those raising the questions are accused of class warfare, despite the fact that economic war has been waged against the poor for generations. But woe to the person who points out the injustice. John Dear, in his book *Peace Behind Bars,* quotes the Roman Catholic Brazilian archbishop Dom Hélder Câmara: "When I feed the hungry, they call me a saint; when I ask why people are hungry, they call me a communist." Those who take up the cause of the poor and powerless are often sidelined and silenced.

Poverty and Inequality

We Friends associate poverty with inequality because one follows the other. Where classes of people are despised and marginalized, they will never enjoy full and equal access to the economic structures that create wealth. Just as inequality breeds poverty, so too does poverty generate inequality. In our cultural myths, the poor and humble person is lionized for his or her faith and virtue, but in reality that person is ignored and ostracized, viewed as a burden to society.

The costs of poverty and inequality are widespread and dramatic. When growing numbers of people are unable to participate in the economy, all are at risk. When some suffer the ill effects of poor education, malnourishment, and unemployment, all people are eventually harmed. Just as a gangrenous limb poses a risk to the entire body, so do sustained and untreated poverty and inequality threaten the wider culture. If only for the most

> In our cultural myths, the poor and humble person is lionized for his or her faith and virtue, but in reality that person is ignored and ostracized, viewed as a burden to society.

selfish of reasons, our own well-being, we should eradicate poverty and inequity wherever they are present.

We must change our minds about poverty and those in it. Too often poverty is viewed as a product of laziness or immorality. I remember my own hard feelings toward a woman who once asked me for money; I ignored the fact that her crippling mental illness prevented full-time employment. On later reflection, I marveled that she had accomplished what she had, then I wondered, were I in her situation, if I would have been as self-sufficient as she.

Some still believe poverty is a sign of God's disfavor, a penalty suffered by those who've disappointed or angered God. The wealthy often speak about how God has blessed them, which implies God has cursed the poor. But much of the vast wealth in our nation has had little to do with God and more to do with human greed, an economic system that has rewarded it, and a political system that has bowed to it.

As for the supposed laziness of the poor, I have seen far more people made indolent by wealth. Time and again, family businesses have been bankrupted by second and third generations so accustomed to ease they could not persevere. Inherited wealth discourages productivity and diligence. Habits of work and industry are forgotten. Though the poor are often accused of having a sense of entitlement, it's been my experience that wealth is far more likely to create an expectation of support and privilege. Many of the wealthy believe their value to society is so great that no restrictions or demands should be placed upon them, lest their wealth, which they claim benefits all, be threatened.

John Woolman, the Quaker prophet, understood the danger of wealth in moral development. When his reputation as a tailor grew, his vocation and wealth claimed a disproportionate amount of his attention, causing his work for justice to suffer. Doing well hampered his ability to do good. His decision to honor equality for all above wealth for himself enabled him to work for the end of slavery, first among Friends, then among the nations.

Of course, I know there are wealthy people who use their resources for great good, who labor to alleviate human suffering. Nevertheless, great wealth is a risk to the soul, causing otherwise moral beings to forsake good to protect and expand their riches. Our attitudes about wealth and the honor we pay it have helped create a society in which equality is lifted up as a virtue, though it is clear some are more equal than others. Unless we challenge the vast financial inequities in our society, and move to separate wealth from equality, democracy is at risk.

Equality and the Search for Truth

Equality lies at the heart of the Quaker's search for truth. To be a Quaker is to believe God is in all persons, and thus God can speak through all persons. This is not to say all persons are equally gifted at discerning truth, only that no person ought to be casually dismissed in our search for truth. For God can speak through whomever God wishes, whenever God wishes, with no regard for the artificial limitations we have placed upon her. Indeed, any theology that limits the voice, activity, and range of God is guilty of the most egregious idolatry—worshipping the golden calf of religion and dogma, having forgotten both the majesty and wideness of God's Spirit. My use of the word *her* when referring to God in this paragraph, and the unease it causes some, demonstrates the human tendency to limit our under-standing of God, thereby hampering our search for truth.

A commitment to spiritual truth carries with it the convic-tion this truth can come from any person or event at any time, usually when we least expect it. Equality asks us to affirm the universality of God's proclamation. We owe it to God, others, and ourselves to listen carefully to all, regardless of their station or status in life. For when we listen only to a like-minded few, our regard for others diminishes, our love for them wanes, and with that our commitment to their equality and well-being lessens.

Love, not status, is the test of when one claims to speak for God. Love was the test for Jesus, and one he commended to us when he asked us to love God and one another. The test of love

> God will never call us to a life or work
> that is anything less than loving.

is the central theme of the Christian life, even though we have at times resisted its broader implications. God will never call us to a life or work that is anything less than loving. I changed my mind about marriage equality when I discerned that denying homosexuals the same blessing of marriage I enjoy was not only selfish but also unloving. I could no longer believe God was honored or pleased by my efforts to deny others the joy of loving, committed relationships. Because the insights and leadings gained in our search for truth must meet the criteria of love, I was able to move beyond an exclusive tradition.

The search for truth calls us forward. Truth never asks us to return to a time or period of lesser enlightenment. It never elevates the flawed past at the expense of a more perfect, more inclusive future. It is not uncommon for people of faith to long for a fabled past. But that past, while glorious in memory, often came at the expense of others, marginalizing a minority so the majority could be blessed. A mutual commitment to love and equality removes our blinders. We are able to see not only the glories of the past but also the inequities, and therefore we have no wish to repeat those injustices or pretend they didn't exist. For people of faith, love and equality are the gateways to all moral, ethical, and spiritual progress, leading us beyond our current perceptions into new lands.

A commitment to love and equality ultimately unites humanity, though initially it might cause division as we resist the higher ethic to which we are being called. Any new perspective is invariably met with resistance, since it often challenges our comfort and status. But its purpose is never to separate the sheep from the goats or the wheat from the chaff. Rather, it seeks to harmonize the disparate elements of the human community. It lets us see where we are apart, where hatred and prejudice have separated us, and works to weave us together into a tapestry in which each thread is valued and crucial to the whole.

Equality and Religion

Regrettably, religion has not always been a friend to equality and justice. I have been involved in organized religion all my life, first as a Roman Catholic, then as a Quaker. I move with ease in religious circles, understand the nuances of religious life, cross denominational boundaries often, engage persons of other religions regularly and happily, and will likely participate in religion the rest of my life. I read the Bible regularly, despite my discomfort with some of its conclusions. In short, religion fascinates me. I have seen in religion goodness and beauty so profound as to be breathtaking. Though I have nothing against humanists or atheists and share many of their conclusions, I am a better person because of religion. It has taught me to care for the poor, to love the unlovable, to seek the best in others, and to forgive. Religion has exposed me to people I likely wouldn't have encountered any other way. Consequently, it has helped me overcome my prejudices, widened my world, and taught me realities and truths different from my own. Religion has given me an appreciation for mystery and wonder, has created in me a desire to know more, and has motivated my movement from gnat-straining legalism to open-handed liberalism. It has transformed me from an American partisan to a citizen of the world. Religion has made me a better son, husband, father, and friend. Most every admirable quality I possess, if I possess any at all, is due in large part to my loving, life-giving religion.

But religion has a shadow side, for it's likely that for every life positively influenced by religion, just as many lives have been diminished by it. Slavery persisted not only because of its perceived economic value but also because many people of faith believed it to be God's will. Wherever war is present, one does not have to look far to find the hand of religion. Today, the chief barrier for full marriage equality for gays and lesbians is religious objections. Just as religion promotes much good, so too does it bring out the worst in some people, blinding them to injustice. Too often, religion has been the last to see the light, the last institution to advance the causes of justice and equality.

This double-mindedness is present in every religion. Each religion contains people who are fearful of moral progress and the change it brings, people who prefer comfortable injustice over the growing pains of righteousness. Mistaking their intransigence for faithfulness, they believe God stands with them. Appeals to their sense of fair play accomplish little, so strong is their certainty of God's will. Sadly, the voice for equality has often been a minority voice within the church. Many denominations reject the leadership of women, while happily taking their money and exploiting their labor. They take full advantage of the spiritual gifts of gays and lesbians, until their sexual orientation becomes known, then are shocked and regretful, announcing their love for the "sinner" and their hate for the "sin."

As wonderful as religion has been for me, I know it could have been otherwise. Had I been born a woman or gay or black, my experience in the church would have been radically different. It is this reality we must resolve to change. To be a Quaker is to commit oneself to thorough and lasting equality. It is to stand with the scorned, the powerless, the friendless, and estranged, especially when the world would turn from them. An unswerving commitment to the Golden Rule is our goal: to treat others with the same dignity, compassion, and respect we wish for ourselves. We believe Jesus Christ, in seeking out the marginalized and despised, exemplified the way of justice and equality. But not Jesus alone, for we have seen and known others who did the same.

To live the Quaker way is to be acutely aware of those benefits enjoyed at the expense of others. It is to create a world where all are valued and respected. Wherever the poor are cast aside, wherever people are scorned, wherever economic systems and governments keep the lowly down, there the faithful and righteous should gather in solidarity.

Because religion has often been the handmaiden of discrimination, those who love both justice and faith must remedy our past errors. If God has a preference for the poor and powerless, and Scripture certainly suggests that to be the case, then the poor must also receive the bulk of our attention and resources. They should be welcomed into our churches as joyfully as the rich and prominent, and they must never be made to feel less valued because of their circumstances. To diminish the poor is to diminish the Jesus who had no place to lay his head.

On any given Sunday at our Quaker meeting, there are a number of visitors. One Sunday, a prominent and powerful man came to worship. After worship, I hurried to introduce myself, trying to win him over, mindful of the gifts he could bring our meeting. That same Sunday, a poorly dressed couple also attended. Though I welcomed them, as I welcome all, I made little effort to learn about them, believing they had nothing to offer us. Later that day, it occurred to me how rudely I had treated them. I hoped they might come back the next Sunday so I could properly welcome them, but they didn't return. What is it like to be overlooked, to be quickly judged and just as quickly dismissed? What is it like to realize your view is valued less than that of others, to realize others won't seek you out, won't welcome you gladly, won't be interested in your perspective? What is it like to discern, at an early age, that the world holds little regard for you?

Any religion that does not have a kind and hopeful word for the world's oppressed or creates by virtue of its principles an underclass is not a religion worth our dedication or obedience. As for me, I want no part of any god or religion that exalts some and vilifies others. Nor will I pledge my support to a government that extends justice to a privileged few. To live the Quaker way is to see God not just in some but in all. It is to want the best for all and to work for that lofty goal with a cheerful heart and unflagging zeal. It is to want what Jesus wanted—God's kingdom of peace and justice to be realized on earth, just as it is realized in heaven. To live the Quaker way is to scorn injustice and reject self-interested privilege. It is, in the words of the prophet Micah, to do justice, love mercy, and walk humbly with the God who cherishes all.

A Quaker Way
Altar Call

I began this book encouraging you to embrace the way of life I've discovered among Friends. I want it to do for you what it has done for me.

In times of moral confusion, living the Quaker way has provided clarity and direction.

When I have been tempted to believe material gain will bring me joy, its clarion call for simple and centered living has cheered my heart.

When I have thought violence and war appropriate solutions to evil and injustice, the Quaker way has reminded me of the power of love and reconciliation.

When I have played fast and loose with the truth, it has taught me to walk the straight line.

When I have been selfish, it has made the joys of community all the more real to me and saved me from self-absorption.

When I have treated some people as lesser, the Quaker way has reminded me of the deep esteem in which God holds all people and has empowered me to work for the good of everyone.

It has reminded me that God speaks to all and through all.

It has taught me to listen more, speak less, and seek the happiness and well-being of others insofar as I am able.

Living the Quaker way has, in every sense, made my life a deep and present joy.

I believe it can do the same for you. For I believe you and I are not all that different, that we struggle with the same problems and challenges common to all. Whether you formally join a Quaker community is secondary to me, as it would be to any other Quaker. It is your embodiment of these ideals that I encourage, for the good of your life, for the good of your soul, for the good of this world. With those high hopes in mind, I invite you to walk and to live this Quaker way.

Living the Quaker Way Through the Queries

Central to the Quaker way is the practice of reflection on one's life. Self-awareness, through honest self-evaluation, helps us embrace the ideals of the transformed life. The Quaker queries are self-directed questions that help us discern our habits, values, and priorities. The following queries were selected to bring a deeper focus on each of the Quaker testimonies: simplicity, peace, integrity, community, and equality. They were gathered from a variety of sources, including Britain Yearly Meeting, Philadelphia Yearly Meeting, Pacific Yearly Meeting, Northwest Yearly Meeting, and Western Yearly Meeting.

I invite you to read one query each day for the next thirty days. Keep it before you. Write it down, and in quiet moments, reflect upon it. Open your life to its challenge and power.

Some persons have found it helpful to gather in small groups to reflect upon and discuss the queries, or to use them as a basis for open, or silent, worship.

DAY 1 Do I live simply and promote the right sharing of the world's bounty?

DAY 2 Do I keep my life uncluttered
with things and activities,
avoiding commitments beyond
my strength and light?

DAY 3 How do I maintain simplicity, moderation, and honesty in my speech, my manner of living, and my daily work?

DAY 4   Do I refuse to let the prevailing
culture and media dictate my
needs and values?

DAY 5 Do I recognize when I have enough?

DAY 6 Do I keep myself informed about
the effects my style of living is
having on the global economy
and environment?

DAY 7 When differences arise, do
I make earnest effort to end
them speedily?

DAY 8   Do I work for the establishment
of alternative ways of settling
disputes?

DAY 9 Am I aware that to build a world community requires that we all face our differences honestly, openly, and in trust?

DAY 10 Do I treat conflict as an
opportunity for growth,
and address it with careful
attention?

DAY 11   Do I look for ways to reaffirm
in action and attitude my love
for the one with whom I am in
conflict?

DAY 12   Where there is distrust, injustice, or hatred, how am I an instrument of reconciliation and love?

DAY 13 How do I manage my
commitments so that
overcommitment, worry,
and stress do not diminish
my integrity?

QUERIES ON INTEGRITY

DAY 14   If pressure is brought upon me to
lower my standard of integrity,
am I prepared to resist it?

DAY 15   Am I truthful and honest in my business transactions, punctual in fulfilling my promises, and prompt in the payment of my debts?

DAY 16   Am I careful to speak truth as I
know it, and am I open to truth
spoken to me?

DAY 17   Am I reflective about the ways
I gain my wealth and income
and sensitive to their impacts
on others?

DAY 18 What unpalatable truths might
I be evading?

DAY 19 Do I consider difficult questions
with an informed mind as well as
a generous and loving spirit?

DAY 20   Do I strive to create a community life that will promote the mental and physical well-being of all concerned?

DAY 21   Am I careful of the reputation
of others?

DAY 22 As a worker, employer, producer, consumer, and investor, do I endeavor to cultivate goodwill and mutual understanding in my economic relationships?

DAY 23 What am I doing to carry my share
of responsibility for the government of our community, nation,
and world?

DAY 24 How do I attend to the suffering of
others in our local community, in
our state and nation, and in the
world community?

DAY 25   Am I alert to practices here and throughout the world which discriminate against people on the basis of who or what they are or because of their beliefs?

DAY 26 Am I open to new light, from whatever source it may come?

DAY 27   Do I examine myself for aspects
of prejudice that may be buried,
including beliefs that seem to
justify biases based on race,
gender, sexual orientation,
disability, class, and feelings
of inferiority or superiority?

DAY 28   What am I doing to help overcome the contemporary effects of past and present oppression?

DAY 29 Am I teaching my children, and do I show through my way of living, that love of God includes affirming the equality of people, treating others with dignity and respect, and seeking to recognize and address that of God within every person?

DAY 30   Do I make my home a place
of friendliness, joy, and peace,
where my family and visitors
feel God's presence?

ACKNOWLEDGMENTS

My journey in the Quaker way began in 1977, when I was invited to attend the Young Friends group at the home of Lee and Mary Lee Comer, our neighbors at the time. I was immediately made to feel welcome. It was the beginning of a transformative pilgrimage. Since then, I have been involved in six Quaker meetings, serving five of them as a pastor. Each meeting contributed positively to my spiritual development. I am indebted not only to Lee and Mary Lee but also to each of the Quaker communities I have known.

Quakers are theologically diverse, and therefore we resist easy description. But Thomas Hamm, the Quaker historian, knows our faith and history better than any living person. He provided helpful assistance as I wrote these reflections, and I am indebted to him.

Fairfield Friends Meeting, the meeting I pastor, was gracious enough to allow me the time necessary to write this book. My co-pastors, Jennifer Silvers and Matt Hamm, shouldered their work and mine. Everyone should be so blessed to be in community with such wonderful Friends.

As always, my wife, Joan Gulley, provided needed encouragement and balance. She is, in all ways, a gift to me. As are my sons, Spencer and Sam.

My faithful dog, Zipper, kept me company during the writing of this book and died at its conclusion. May I be the kind of person she thought I was.

Philip regularly enjoys speaking at churches, colleges, libraries, retreats, and conventions around the country. If you would like to schedule Philip to speak to your group or organization, please send an e-mail inquiry to **speechinfo@philipgulley.com** or visit **www.philipgulley.com** for a list of his upcoming appearances.

If you are interested in receiving Philip's weekly messages, you may sign up to receive his GraceTalks newsletter at www.philipgulley.com.